Living With Simplicity
& Discovering What Matters

Marie A. Laverriere

LivingWithSimplicity.com

Living With Simplicity & Discovering What Matters
2025 © Marie A. Laverriere
ISBN 978-1-7362908-3-5

Cover photo by Marie A. Laverriere

Geraldine Aikman, cover and book designer

Genie Dailey, editor

Marie A. Laverriere, publisher
www.LivingWithSimplicity.com

I dedicate this book
to my friend Dave

CONTENTS

ABOUT THE AUTHOR

I thought it would be more informative if I started this book with an introduction of myself and a bit about my life so that you would have an understanding of why I chose to write this book. Also, I wanted to share some major points in my experience toward living with simplicity. In other words, what was the process that got me to this place in my life. I know that I appreciate it when authors share some information about themselves when I read their books so I have a context in which to better understand their perspectives.

Let me begin with a story from a long time ago when I was a child. I remember imagining a tiny white cottage in my backyard at home. I remember that it had two front windows with flower boxes, and the door was open and I saw a bed, a table, and a chair, and it felt to me that it had everything I needed to live in this small space. The feelings I had were cozy, peaceful, and I wished at the time that I could move into it. Inevitably, of course, I forgot about it and went on with my life.

I was married at 18 years old, and we eventually had three children. My first daughter was born when I was 21 and my second daughter was born when I was 23; my son came to us a few years later. They all live locally with a total of eight grandchildren. In my busy life, I forgot how much I had enjoyed imagining living in that tiny cottage. Life happened, and the idea of living a simple life got put on hold for many years.

I divorced after 33 years of marriage, and for the first time in my life I was alone. I left the house we had bought and rented several apartments over the years. I was born and had lived in Southern Maine most of my life except for the seven years when I lived in Albuquerque, New Mexico. When I came back to Maine from New Mexico in May of 2016, I had to start over from the beginning, find a job then a place to live and so forth. I had hired a moving company to move all my furniture and other possessions back to Maine and this cost me a lot of money. After I found work, I eventually found an apartment by the river in Southern Maine. I lived in this apartment for a little less than three years.

Then I met a person who became a very good friend, and he owns property on the southern coast of Maine. He has ten small cottages ranging from 200+ to 400+ square feet in size. He told me to look at all of them, and if I liked one and was interested in renting from him, I could have it. This property is located right across the street from the ocean/beach…of course I was interested! When I first saw the cottage that I now live in, it reminded me of the imaginative cottage from my youth. The cottage has two front windows with flower boxes, and it measures 293 square feet. The bonus part is that it's located across the street from the ocean. I love walking on the beach—it's probably my favorite thing to do—and I never thought I could ever afford to live on the coast.

We usually need some motivation to declutter our possessions, and this tiny cottage located 100 steps from the ocean was the fuel that helped me purge 95 percent of my possessions. I remembered that I had paid $5,000 to move all my things from New Mexico to Maine, and now I was giving almost everything away! If I had known what my future held, I would have sold all my furniture in New Mexico and brought with me only what I could fit in my car. The saying goes "live and learn," and so I did, at a cost; however, the outcome has been wonderful.

I knew how many things I could bring with me to the cottage that would fit without looking cramped. I had several weeks to go through everything I owned and get rid of everything I did not absolutely need. I used my five shelving units (6 feet high by 3 feet wide by 11 inches deep) that I knew would fit in the cottage. At the time, these were the bookshelves where I kept about 2,000 or more books. I used these units as my guide to what I could bring with me into the cottage. I went through all my possessions three times. It was not easy to do this because I had to really let go of many things that

2

I had thought I needed at one time or another in my life. I used the mantra "if I did not use it this past year then I don't need it." I gave away almost all my furniture, a lot of clothing, and many other things.

My friend offered to help me move with his pickup truck, and I filled my Honda CRV, and off we went with everything I now owned. The feeling of having so little in possessions was freeing and wonderful. After we unloaded everything, my friend looked at the stacks of boxes we had placed in the cottage and said, "You'll never fit all of this in here," and I said yes I will—and I did, and it did not look cluttered or cramped. A very handy tip when living in a small space is to have shelving units as I mentioned above: Because of their measurements, they fit right against the wall, and they hardly take any space because the shelves are only 11 inches deep. I used decorative boxes and baskets to store almost everything in my shelving units. The cottage also has a 19-inch-wide closet with a door as well as shelves built into the wall between the kitchen and the room. These measure 25 inches wide and deep. There are four of them and they are behind a louver door. I use one of the shelf for my clothing, the top one for my essential oil products, and eventually I utilized the other two for work items.

Not long after I moved into the cottage, COVID came upon us. I had an office a few miles away (I'm a licensed clinical social worker and offer mental health therapy and life coaching), so when our governor told us to work from home, I moved my office into my tiny cottage and offered Telehealth sessions to my clients. About two years later I decided to give up my office and continue to work from home permanently. I brought my back-supportive work chair from my office to my cottage, and I gave away everything else that was in my office. I bought a foldable rack for my computer and phone so I could work from home. I also bought two small locking file boxes for the confidential paperwork I had brought with me to the cottage.

I kept everything in my cottage the way it was for almost five years. This past year, 2024, I invested in three slightly larger shelving units with doors to replace the old units. The cottage looks so much calmer because the open shelves with boxes and baskets had a busy look—too much stimulation. When I bought the new units, I also bought a workbench (41 inches wide by 20 inches deep by 39 inches high) and a stool. My friend is very handy, and he took my very comfortable office chair and made it into a stool with some of the pieces from the new stool. This workbench fits perfectly in my space, and it gives me a good-size surface to both work on and do my art. My friend also bought me a larger storage unit for outside my cottage, replacing the smaller one I'd had for seasonal storage. With this new one, I was now able to store my e-bike and other items like the wooden trunk that I had removed from inside the cottage to make space for the new workbench.

After I first moved into the tiny cottage, I worked on decluttering other aspects of my life. Just one example is that I decluttered my finances. Sometimes we don't realize that knowing the reality of our financial situation is the key to having freedom to choose how we want to live. If my expenses were equal to or less than my income, I was able to be at peace with living my life the way I wanted to. However, if my expenses were more than my income, then I was in debt and I needed to fix it. I was in debt when I moved into the cottage. My solution was to work more hours and pay off my credit cards and car loan as well as other loans. Then when I worked on lowering the cost of my cell phone, internet service, and car insurance, as well as limiting my shopping for things that I did not need, I could live on working fewer hours. And, I'd have more time to enjoy my life doing other things that makes me happy and spending time with people who love and support me. I will write more about decluttering other aspects of life later in the book. I have an entire chapter and worksheet on managing finances.

I felt so happy about my experience of moving into this tiny cottage and allowing myself to live a more simple life that I decided to write a book titled *Minimalism for Well-Being: A Guide to*

Simplifying All Facets of Your Life. I published the book on Amazon in 2021. This book has a lot of information on how I decluttered my possessions (step by step) and other parts of my life. It invites the reader to reflect on their own desires to declutter and simplify their lives. Soon after I published this first book, I decided to write and publish a second one titled *A Journey to Authenticity: Finding Freedom, Peace, & Joy.* I had time to reflect on the non-physical parts of my life and the many lessons I had learned over the years, as well as all the blessings I was able to experience, and this is basically what this book is about.

After almost five and a half years of living a simple life in this wonderful tiny cottage and enjoying walks on the beach almost daily, I'm beginning to think about the rest of my life. I plan to retire at the end of 2025. I've been working since I was 14 years old and I'll be almost 70. For me, being retired means having more time to do things that fuel my passion. It's having more time to express my creativity and what has meaning in my life and to practice self-care. It's time to receive a paycheck (social security) every month without worrying if the insurance companies will pay me on time or not.

I embrace the thought of living with simplicity, and as I practice it, I feel that it's part of my spiritual connection to what gives my life meaning. It has been a process which began when I was invited by a friend to rent one of his cottages. I strongly believe that living with simplicity can occur whether a person lives in a tiny home or a huge mansion; it isn't the size of your home that allows you to live with simplicity, but rather it is the choices one makes in how they live.

Living with simplicity continues to be my life practice in all the areas of my existence. I call it a practice because it's a process. And some processes have no end. It's like a perpetual journey. I do not have a roadmap, so my choice to live with simplicity is an adventure. Living with simplicity provides us the opportunity to remove the layers of things that distract us in life and to connect with what is most important.

As I mentioned above, I am an LCSW, and I have provided mental health therapy for the past 21 years. I've met with many people who suffer from anxiety. I truly believe that when we choose a lifestyle of living with simplicity, we are more able to connect to ourselves and our inner wisdom/intuition, and our quality of life usually enriches—instead of being in the rat race of life where most people end up (I'm not judging; I've been there). We don't always know that we have the freedom to make other choices, but people living with simplicity know they have choices, and they can take the time to be in the present moment and make healthy decisions. I chose to have a slower pace to my life because when I am rushed for whatever reasons, I feel anxious and annoyed. A slower pace that fits our needs is important to our well-being. All of this may help lessen anxiety in a person.

When I was 25, a friend of mine asked me, "Marie, are you happy?" I remember thinking, what kind of questions is that? I had never thought about being happy or considered it a choice in my life. I responded with a very long *yesss*…with a question mark at the end. I realized after he asked me this question and I had time to ponder that my real answer was that I was not happy. I do want to say that I loved having children and enjoyed them thoroughly, but other aspects of my life were not easy. I had lived my life until then never knowing that I had the freedom to choose what I wanted in my life. My maternal grandmother and parents all told me how I should live my life, and that is what I did. In my sophomore year of high school, I had asked my parents about the possibility of going to college. My parents told me that college was for boys, not girls, and that girls get married and have children. I did not even question my parents' answer or explore whether I had other options. By the way, there were never any boys who went to college in my entire extended family until 35 years later. It is very difficult for people to go against the grain of familiarity or family traditions. My parents had no clue that a college education could benefit a woman.

The same person who had asked me if I was happy (I never told him that I was not happy after I figured it out), five years later encouraged me to go to college. I was 30 years old at that time. He explained to me that there were grants and loans that we could avail ourselves of if we could not afford to pay the tuition outright. So, I went to college for 20 years (while working and taking care of my family) and earned a bachelor's degree and a master's in Social Work, as well as a master's and a doctorate in Pastoral Ministry. With the two last degrees, my concentration was always in spirituality. I had the privilege of working at very interesting positions in my life, including as a member of the State of Maine House of Representatives and being an Interfaith Chaplain at a county jail in Albuquerque, New Mexico, and I have the pleasure of being self-employed as an LCSW in private practice for the last ten years. My education benefited me in ways I could never have dreamed of.

My life was far from simple until I moved into the cottage on the coast of Maine. I'd always had a desire to simplify my life, but it was buried very deeply in my psyche. I have a belief that everyone desires some simplicity in their lives just for the sake of remaining sane, but unless we have an opportunity and decide to start the process of living with simplicity, it won't happen. I hope my story helps you become interested in thinking about (if you haven't done so already) starting to imagine a more simple life for yourself.

I come to the end of my story (so far), and I am excited to share some tools that I have found useful in the different areas where one can start to or continue to declutter one's life and practice the art of living with simplicity. And I can honestly say that I am happy. If that old friend would ask me that question today, I would respond with conviction and certainty that I am truly happy in my life.

INTRODUCTION

In living my life with simplicity, I came to the understanding that we all come to it in our own individual ways. It's a personal journey that allows us to tap into the layers of our lives and connect with what is most important. Furthermore, it's an ongoing process that does not end but rather enlightens us further as we decide to continue. Some people find their way in beginning this process early on in life, and others find their way at a later age. The most important thing is that we find our path to living with simplicity at some point in our lives if only to experience the peace, calm, and joy that comes with it.

In this world today, everything seems to be changing quickly and at times feels a bit scary because some of the events we are experiencing are not positive. Living with simplicity seems to offer a viable path to feeling some peace because it helps us reconnect with who we are and tap into our inner wisdom for guidance—and to embrace the power we have in being true to ourselves.

In this book, I will share with you some information that has been helpful to me on my journey to living with simplicity. I will offer opportunities for you to reflect on different aspects of your life and reconnect, or connect more fully, to who you are. I begin by inviting you to think about everything, everyone, and all events and activities that you value in your life. This reflection may give you snippets of information that can help you come to know yourself more clearly. In the second chapter we ponder the question "Who am I?"— very complex question yet extremely relevant if we desire to be happy.

Another aspect of importance that I cover in this book is having knowledge of our financial status so that we can live our lives fully and free to make choices in creating the life we desire. I mentioned some information on finances in "About the Author," but I will say more in Chapter Three, and I have a worksheet available at the end of the chapter. Our use of time will also be examined because time is one of our greatest resources: It has an expiration date, and then we leave this planet, so we need to use it to the best of our ability.

A famous German spiritual writer named Eckhart Tolle once said that people's worst enemy is usually found between their ears. I'm paraphrasing, but I'm certain he was referring to our thoughts. I have a theory about how our thoughts are created.

We have accumulated our thoughts since we were born (and for some of us, that is many years of accumulation), and they are at times very deeply ingrained within us, and sometimes they are negative and cause us pain. After I moved into my cottage and decluttered several aspects of my life, I started working on decluttering my negative thoughts and replacing them with positive ones, and I found this process very difficult. For me, it was probably the most difficult of all to declutter. I pondered why it was so difficult, and I came to believe that our accumulated thoughts form our perspectives of ourselves, others, and the world. Our perspectives form our beliefs (the rules we live our lives by). And ultimately, our perspectives (whether they are accurate or not) and beliefs affect our behaviors. In *Living With Simplicity*, I share tools to help us manage our thoughts—to enable us to change the negative ones into positive ones so our lives may become more joyful and peaceful.

We are all having a human experience, and it's very important that we care for our health in as many ways as we can. I share some basic information on how to do this in Chapter Eight.

Human beings have a need to find meaning in life. Some people find meaning in nature, some in spiritual practices, others in religion, and most find meaning in creative expressions where we allow our passions to flow and our hearts to sing, and we are able to give a voice to our souls on this planet. I will say more on these and invite you to reflect on your own path to finding meaning in your life as well as explore what creative expressions speak to you.
I believe that we are spiritual beings having a human experience, so we must also tend to our spirit being, and we can do this by nurturing what gives our lives meaning and by taking the time to find and express our creativity.

I have a chapter on how to move forward when you seek to live with simplicity. I begin by defining what decluttering is and sharing easy steps to accomplish it. We all live a "simple life" differently, so I suggest ideas to help you get started. I wrote Chapter Nine in hopes that it would make it easier for people to take their first steps. I understand that some of you have already started this process, so take from this chapter whatever is helpful to you.

The last chapter is for those of us who are older, seniors, and the different issues we sometimes have to deal with that we may not have been told about. Our society values productivity and youth, and when we age, our pace of life must slow down to accommodate our quality of life. Some people find this difficult because, again, society does not value slowing down. So I include in this chapter possible challenges that we may experience and how to work with them and still have a wonderful life. If you are not a senior, you probably know someone who is, and this information may be helpful to you in better understanding their experiences.

As I mentioned before, at the end of most chapters I offer a worksheet with a variety of tools to help those who want to work on specific issues in the process of simplifying their lives. The information in this book comes from years of experience in my own life, as well as my experience as a clinical social worker meeting with clients on their life journeys. I continue to learn new ways of living with simplicity and finding peace and joy in my life, so this book is not complete but simply a beginning.

Please purchase a blank journal and use it to answer the questions in each chapter and on the worksheets. When we actually write down our thoughts, studies have shown that we are better able to remember and process the information more deeply.

Also, I want to thank you for being interested in exploring *living with simplicity & discovering what matters*. I hope the information is helpful to you on your journey. *Marie*

CHAPTER ONE

What Do I Value in My Life?

To acknowledge what we value in our lives and include this knowledge in our daily life is to have an understanding of what we are grateful for in our everyday living.

What I Value in My Life

Creating a list of every thing, person, and event that I value in my life begins the process of knowing myself.

To know what I value allows me to begin to understand what is important to me.

It is consequential that I incorporate all the items on my list into my life.

In doing so, I honor myself and tend to my dearest desires of what I truly value.

Before we define who we are and reflect on being true to ourselves, it is important to know what and who we value in our lives. This activity gives us hints and a clearer picture in helping us know who we are and what possessions we want to keep before we start to simplify and/or declutter our space(s) and the other areas in our lives that need change. It is important to examine what we value in our everyday living. I'm not referring to our values but rather ***what*** we value.

In my many years of working with people, I have realized that numerous individuals have lost touch with themselves and with knowing what they value in their lives—what gives them joy and happiness or allows their passion to flow and their hearts to sing. One of my discoveries is that when individuals are caregivers for many years, they sometimes give it their all and have nothing left for themselves, so they lose touch with who they are and what they value in their lives. Others never knew that they had choices in finding what they valued, so they never reflected on it. The bottom line is that we all have the responsibility to reflect upon, think about, and come to know what we value in our lives so that we can create opportunities to include them on a daily basis. It's a roadmap to creating the life we desire as well as knowing ourselves better, which in turn allows us the ability to live with simplicity.

I offer a tool to help us seriously examine what we value in our lives in the areas of **things** (including emotions), **people** (only the ones who love and support us—and are not afraid to call us out [from a place of love] and accept us just the way we are), and **events/activities**. These three areas can be described in three lists. Let me give you a few examples from my own lists so that you will understand the very simple things you may value as well as the more complex ones. I value my two cups of coffee with half-and-half cream every morning. I love the taste of coffee with cream. I drink unsweetened cold brew, and I purchase it at the grocery store. It comes in 48-ounce containers. Cold brew has 70% less acid than regular coffee, and since I have a problem with acid reflux, this coffee is perfect for me. I also value a comfortable mattress and pillow and my duvet; a daily shower with strong water pressure and lots of hot water; and the ability to follow a very slow pace in my morning routine. I also value my dog and his wonderful calm and quiet presence in the morning.

These are a few ideas of what one might put on their list of **things** they value—the simple stuff. We can also add bigger things: For example, I enjoy living in a tiny cottage by the ocean so I can take walks on the beach every day. I enjoy having a hybrid car because I use less gasoline. In this category, I also encourage you to name the emotions that you value in your life. For instance, I value the feelings of peace and calm, and I try really hard to avoid anything or anyone who threatens my experience of these emotions. I share these ideas with you to help you come up with your own. Sometimes when we start thinking of things we value, we get stuck in the big things, so sharing my simple ones is my way of suggesting that you really think about what makes you happy in the simpleness of life.

The second list consists of all the **people** that we value in our lives. Please try not to put everyone you know or are related to on this list. Do not feel guilty for choosing only the ones you truly value; no one else needs to see your list. Put only the people who love you unconditionally and support you and accept you as you are. These are the people you love spending time with. Make sure that you do make the time to meet with these people regularly. This list is a bit difficult at times because there may be people whom you want on your list, but they don't want to be in a relationship with you, so in these cases, you need to avoid placing them on your list. We have no control over other people; we only have control over our own decisions and actions. My people list currently has four individuals. These lists change over time. We are always assessing what and who we value, and life is not stagnant—it is forever changing. Therefore, our lists will most probably change over time, and that is to be expected.

The third list consists of **events and activities** that we value in our lives. Events and activities both have a participation component, but sometimes activities allows us to be more involved than events. What I mean is that an event can be a concert or a movie where we sit and watch. Other examples are going to a restaurant, attending a class, or gathering with friends. Activities are more participatory, like a walk, playing a game, cooking dinner, practicing yoga, meditating, dancing, taking photographs, or creating art. Sometimes it's difficult to define something as either an activity or an event because they are closely related and some can fall into either category. It does not matter; just list all the things you enjoy doing and that you value as part of your life. In the activity section I include being creative. I have devoted an entire chapter to the definition, description, and very important aspects of creative expressions that one can engage in. The creative activities that we value doing in our lives are very important to include on this list.

An important point to remember when creating your lists is that they don't have to be in order of importance. Just brainstorm the ideas in whatever order they come to you. Ponder seriously what you truly value in your life and put them on your three lists. Since they are all important, you need to find ways to incorporate each of them in your life regularly, and if they are new, add them to your life as soon as you can.

We are the creators of our lives. And yes, sometimes things happen that we did not plan or want, but we must move through those moments as best we can, often with help from people we trust, and then return to experiencing the things, people, and events we value in our lives. An example for me is that several months after my first book was published, my six-and-a-half-year-old dog, Rumi, who is pictured on the back cover of the book, died of cancer. He was fine one day, and the next day we were told that he was full of cancer. We tried different therapies without success, and he died eighteen days later. My friend was so supportive to both my dog and me, I'm not sure how I could have made it through without his support. I continued taking daily walks on the beach with my friend as we both grieved the loss of Rumi.

I want to add a short reflection on "being happy" as part of what we value in our lives. The question is: "Are you happy?" I truly believe that we are supposed to be happy in this lifetime. There are moments when we have difficult things happen, and I am not denying that life brings about challenges. Being happy, however, is part of being alive and experiencing the flow of our passion as we allow ourselves to be real. When I was young and immersed in religious teachings, I was led to believe that suffering was our plight, but I later discovered that being happy was our true birthright, and that realization changed my entire approach to life. When we choose to work in areas that we have passion for and/or have creative expressions that bring us joy, then we experience purpose and meaning, and this can make us happy. Furthermore, simply valuing the relationship we have with ourselves is cause for feeling happy because the most important relationship you will ever have is with yourself.

WORKSHEET ONE
What Do I Value in My Life?

Make three lists.

1. With this first list, write down every**thing** you value in your life. Include all the **emotions** that you value as well. Don't worry about making your list in order of importance; just brainstorm all the things and emotions you value in your life and write them down. The small things and the big things.

2. On the second list, put every **person** you value in your life—the people who love and accept you just the way you are. You love being with these people and look forward to seeing, talking with, and spending time with them. These people call you out on things when they need to be helpful to you with love. Please don't feel guilty for not including all your "friends" and relatives. Be honest with yourself and only include the people whom you truly value in your life.

3. With this third list, you will think about all the **events and activities** that you value in your life. Again, include the simple things and the bigger ones. List them all.

You may have to take a few days to complete these three lists. You really want them to be complete for now. Things do change over time, but for now, make your lists honest and true. If there are some things, people, or events/activities that you already have as part of your life, continue to make time for them. If you have added new ones, make an effort to include them in your life as soon as you can.

A note on people in your life: Avoid listing people whom you want in your life, but who do not choose to be in your life.

CHAPTER TWO

Who Am I?

I am original, no one else is like me, so in this lifetime I must figure out who I am so I can be me and truly appreciate as well as enjoy and share my discoveries and always be open to grow.

Freedom to Be Ourselves

There comes a time in our lives when we believe that we must be free to be ourselves.
It occurred to me that embracing who I am is one of my life lessons.
If I am not able to authentically be myself, then I am not living my potential.
We are all gifted with living out our purpose(s), and in doing so we bless the world.

If we have the desire to live with simplicity, it's important to connect to our true selves, so let us begin with defining ourselves through our many roles and the many hats we wear in our daily living. We will then reflect from the core of our being to discover our true selves. In the process of defining ourselves we discover our complexities, and when we can open our hearts to this discovery, we realize that we are more than physical: We also have an essence of spirit. I'm sharing my belief that we are spiritual beings having a human experience (I write more about this in Chapter Six). I don't expect everyone to believe what I believe, but my invitation to you is to figure out who you are by reflecting on what your beliefs are so that you will have a better understanding of yourself. Sometimes people believe that their physicalness is everything that defines them, and that is perfectly acceptable. So, in this chapter, truly ponder and reflect on who you are so that when difficult things happen in your life, you will have a foundation of knowing yourself that can help you get through the challenges and keep your sense of self intact.

As we begin exploring our roles, we recognize that we do have choices in the roles we have, and so the first step is to reflect on what they are, then we can make changes if we want to. We can eliminate the ones that we no longer want or the ones that do not fit who we are. We can also add new ones if we feel the desire to do so. Remember that you are more than your roles in your life.

Have you ever explored the many roles that you have in your life? The many hats you wear? Have you found yourself realizing that you have some roles that you have no idea how you inherited? Are there any roles you have that other people think you should live out differently than you believe you should? These are all questions that I asked myself when I started exploring my roles. Some roles we have for a while, then we don't have them anymore. An example is my role as daughter. Both my parents have died, so now I am no longer daughter. Other roles change over time. When we have children and they are young, our role as parent is more intense than when our children are adults and (usually) on their own. My roles as granddaughter and niece have ended as well, but I have fond memories of my expired roles.

Sometimes our roles don't turn out the way we expected, so we have to make **adjustments to our expectations**. Let me define what I mean by expectations. It can be as simple as expecting our family members to act a certain way because that is the way we remember them to be, historically speaking. Expectations can really be painful if we can't change them because other people are involved, and we can't control others' behaviors and decisions. Lately, I have come to understand that expectations of ourselves or others can cause us pain if we can't adjust them. Perhaps lowering or changing our expectations are healthy ways in allowing ourselves to experience simplicity. If we are able to change our expectations to match what is happening, especially when we don't have a say in how things are, we are better able to maintain being happy. When we can't make adjustments to our expectations, we may suffer from the pain of wondering why things are as they are and long for them to be different. I am learning to lower or remove my expectations when it is in my best interest to do so. An example might be when an older parent finds it difficult to deal with their adult children because they don't keep in touch. That parent can either love their children the way they are and stop expecting them to be someone they are not, or they can struggle with the way things are and feel badly. We do not have control over other people's ways of living.

Adjusting our expectations is a great self-care tool that allows us to feel at peace with reality. It's a tool that gives us the freedom to change our mindset, to be more in sync with what is. I call these moments "mind adjustments." When we can actually think about what just happened—what might have been painful to us—and rethink it, we can allow ourselves to make an adjustment of our expectations. Sometimes this lets us see the situation from a different perspective and helps minimize the bad feeling(s).

The last part of this process is to remember who we are and appreciate ourselves. We can't change the behaviors of others, but we can choose our thoughts and replace bad feeling(s) by remembering who we truly are. The way that other people treat us does not define who we are. It mostly gives us information on how they see their world. It usually has nothing to do with us personally. Remember that you are a powerful being with qualities and giftedness. Take a moment to embrace your true self. Then accept who the other person is, just the way they are, and don't own their garbage. There are times when we need to distance ourselves from other people whom we feel are toxic to us.

I have touched upon this already and I will mention it again in the chapter on finding meaning in our lives: I believe that we are spiritual beings having a human experience. That is, your true self is the spiritual being part; the human part is for our journey on this planet for a limited time. When I write about embracing your true self, I mean your spirit self that is all good and pure and available to you through your intuition, the voice of your spirit. An easy way to imagine what your intuition is could be described as your "gut feelings." We all have them, and when we listen to our gut feelings, we usually make the right decisions.

After reflecting on the quote at the beginning of this chapter and reviewing your many roles, use your journal to document all your thoughts and to reflect upon and describe who you are. You can make adjustments to your roles, cancel some or change them, or even add some. But most importantly, explore your own beliefs through the possibility of finding meaning in a connection to your spirit self. It's very important to know who we are so that we do not lose our sense of self in difficult life events. When life brings us difficult episodes, they are learning opportunities. My motto is, "lessons are blessings, and they usually help us grow," At other times, the difficulty has nothing to do with us and we need to let it go. See Worksheet Two after this chapter to further explore your understanding of yourself—who you are.

I have a few other points that I think fit right in this chapter. The first one is a short reflection on the words "be true to yourself." This statement, I am told, is the only law that the Yurok Indians have. They believe that if a person is true to him- or herself, they honor not only themselves but everyone else.

When I started to work on being true to myself, I realized that it takes courage to live this way. To be courageous is to have the nerve to stand alone and know that our truth is important enough not to compromise anymore, not to settle for less any longer. We have the freedom to make choices in our lives that we believe to be right for us. Making changes in one's life takes courage because there may be a cost. An example of the cost may be that some of our family and friends believe that we should not make decisions in ways they don't agree with. Courage to be our true selves also does not allow us to wear masks or pretend to be someone other than ourselves. Courage is the essence of tapping into our inner wisdom and truly following the wisdom given. When we allow ourselves to be brave and try new things and attempt to make a difference in this world, then we have courage, even if no one notices. I also believe that if we don't take risks to be true to ourselves, we will feel dis at ease and perhaps experience disease of one type or another.

In the process of being true to ourselves, we must also learn and come to terms with loving the person we are. Yes, loving and honoring ourselves. Respecting who we are and finding ways to spend time with ourselves doing fun things. Treating ourselves to food, events, and activities that make us happy. Once we are able to be comfortable in our own skin, comfortable with who we are, and love ourselves just as we are, then we have arrived at being true to ourselves. Once we can love ourselves unconditionally, we attract people into our lives who are healthy. I strongly believe that if a person cannot love himself or herself, they cannot truly love anyone else.

The last point in this chapter that I feel is important to address is having healthy self-esteem. I have a favorite quote that speaks to having good self-esteem: "A bird sitting on a tree is never afraid of the branch breaking because her trust is not on the branch but in her own wings. Always believe in yourself" (author unknown). The bird trusts itself through its own wings to keep it safe. The definition of self-esteem, according to the New Oxford American Dictionary, is: "self-esteem is having confidence in one's own worth or abilities; self-respect." When we experience healthy self-esteem, we feel able to live our lives with positive thoughts and the knowledge that we are qualified to make intelligent decisions that will bring about results that we are hoping for.

Good self-esteem is closely related to having the ability to be happy. I believe that it is very difficult for us to tap into our intuition, our inner wisdom, if we have low self-esteem, so it is important to work on helping it become healthy. See Worksheet Eight for more information on raising one's self-esteem.

WORKSHEET TWO
Who Am I?

Below, I have a list of questions that may be helpful to you in defining who you are. You may have also answered questions while reading Chapters One and Two, and you can blend all this information. After you review the questions and answer them, write a paragraph that describes the person you are. Remember that we are all works in progress; therefore, the paragraph you will write is who you are today. Be honest and thankful.

-What are my qualities, challenges, and interests?

-What have I accomplished in my life so far that I am proud of?

-What do I value about myself physically, emotionally, mentally, spiritually?

-What do I do well at work? at home? with friends? with family?

-What do I enjoy in my life?

-What do I struggle with in my life?

-Are there parts of me that I do not like? If so, what are they?

-Do I define myself only through the bad experiences that I have had in my life?

-Think about your roles—the ones you chose to have and the ones you were assigned by other people in your life. What are all your roles, and how do they define who you are?

-Are there roles that I want to change or get rid of?

-Are there roles that I want to add?

-Describe the person you want to be.

-Do I believe that there is a spiritual aspect of who I am?

-If so, can I define it more fully?

-What gives my life meaning?

After answering all the questions above, describe who you are in a paragraph!

It is a difficult task to define ourselves with words. However, it can be helpful for us to see on paper our reflections on some ideas of who we believe ourselves to be. In doing so, we begin to tap into our own self-awareness. It is in self-awareness that we truly begin to know who we are.

CHAPTER THREE

My Finances

The standard of success in life isn't how much money you have or how large your house is or how fancy your car is. It is absolutely the amount of joy you feel! —Author Unknown

When we know the status of our finances, we are free to live our lives in a realistic way. Without the facts of our total expenses versus our income, we live our lives as if we are financially blind. I'm mostly intending to share this information with people who are not wealthy—most wealthy people have professionals who take care of their finances and keep them abreast of their financial status. In this chapter, I'm focusing on people who make enough money to live comfortably by utilizing their money wisely, as well as people who live paycheck to paycheck or people who have limited income.

There are people who have shared with me over the years that they live in fear of not having enough money to make ends meet. When I ask these people if they know their expenses and how those expenses relate to their income, most of them have no idea. They have never sat down and looked at the facts of their finances. Some of these people are younger and working full-time, and others are semiretired or fully retired. These people may be working at jobs they hate because they fear that if they search for work that they would enjoy doing, they would not have enough money to live. So, they spend a lot of their limited time on this planet working in positions they do not enjoy because they fear the unknowns of their financial situation.

Some people make more money than they need but have no

quality of life because they work long hours needlessly. Some people spend more money than they make, and they need to know this so they can make changes to fix the situation before it is too late and they are heavily in debt. When I challenge some of these people to sit down and examine their financial status, they panic because they don't know where to start. Sometimes I offer to help them during our therapy sessions to make their expense list and compare it to their income because I believe that knowing the connection between expenses and income can be a way of lowering their anxiety.

Until I was in my early sixties, I always had a very bad feeling when I thought about my finances. It all started when I was a young child and my parents shared with me their financial difficulties. I was the eldest of six children, and I worried about money from a very young age. When I was fourteen, I started working summers, and I was able to save enough money to purchase all my clothing and other expenses that I incurred during the course of the year. My parents housed me, fed me, and provided me with medical and dental attention when I needed it, and I was able to provide for all my other financial needs. I do want to add that my parents loved me and gave me emotional support throughout my youth despite their issues with money.

I do believe that many people have a "thing" with money. They either fear not having enough or worry about something going wrong (an emergency) that may cause them financial hardship. There is a lot of research concerning Americans and money, and unfortunately, the studies have found that most people live from paycheck to paycheck and have no savings for emergencies. Lately, financial studies have found that many Americans have high credit card debt, and we all know that interest rates have been high, especially in the last few years.

Taking an inventory of our expenses and knowing what our financial picture looks like is a wonderful way to take charge of our financial status. For example, we all have to pay for a place to live, a cell phone, access to the internet, a car (including gasoline and other car costs to keep it on the road), and we all have to eat. Most of us also have several other expenses such as medication, health insurance, and so on. Once we have a list of our monthly expenses (some are yearly, so we divide them by 12 for a monthly total), we have knowledge that allows us to make choices. After we examine our expense list, we may be able to eliminate a few of them because we no longer need them. The other way to help lower expenses is to shop around to find the best deals. I did this with my internet, cell phone, and car insurance. Another way I lower my expenses is by planning my meals weekly and making a shopping list, and this helps me to purchase just what I need—so I do not have much waste with food. I also studied the cost of buying coffee at a coffee shop once a day, every day. Then I looked at the cost of buying that same coffee in beans and making it at home. The savings for the same identical coffee was over $1,000 a year! If you do this for 10 years, you will have saved $10,000. Food for thought.

I keep my monthly expenses listed on an index card with the due dates, and I make certain that everything gets paid when it's due (avoiding late fees). The items that I pay once a year, I divide by 12 months and keep track of when they are due. I have no surprises except when the car breaks down or I hit a curb with my tire and split it open (which I did last month). I do keep a small financial cushion for these types of unplanned costs. It is important to be responsible with our income/money. If we know that our income and expenses are pretty close to the same amount, then we need to be smart about not wasting money on things we do not absolutely need.

If our relationship with money is positive, we are responsible with its use (we keep our expenses at or less than our income), and we have a grateful heart when we pay our bills, then money will not be a problem in our lives. I wrote affirmations to help me get rid of my fear of not having enough money to live. It took me a few years to finally feel comfortable with my income versus my expenses.

I did shop around and tried to find the best deals for the things I needed, and I ended up saving quite a bit of money in the process. Positive thoughts usually bring about positive outcomes. Remember that having knowledge of your financial situation gives you great power and the freedom to make wonderful choices in your life. As in everything, we have to be responsible in the way we manage our money, but being open to positive thoughts about having more than enough money can help us attract a flow of income that fits our needs.

A note about how I came to lose my fear of not having enough money in my life. The first thing I did was to write affirmations (see Worksheet Three at the end of this chapter). The next thing I did was to list my expenses and compare them to my income. I wanted to pay off all my credit cards, my car loan, and my furniture loan. I worked extra hours for a few years. I paid my monthly bills, and with the extra money, I started paying off my debts, beginning with the ones with higher interest. When all my debt with credit cards, car, and furniture loans were paid, I re-evaluated my expenses and compared the total to my income. I then knew that I could work fewer hours and pay my expenses easily. I also started to save as much money as I could while keeping a lifestyle that felt comfortable for me.

I developed a mindset that I had everything I needed in clothing because I created my "perfect" wardrobe with clothing I love to wear, and I have enough clothing for all occasions that I can possibly need (until I wear them out and buy new ones). I did the same thing with my kitchen items and with household cleaning and personal hygiene products so I never have the urge to "go shopping" as a fun activity. I prevent myself from roaming stores and looking at items I do not need. When I do need clothing, I make a plan for buying it, and I do not deprive myself of what I need. An example is when I had my total shoulder joint replacement surgery this past year and had to purchase new pants that were easier to put on with my weak and painful shoulder. I bought five pairs of elastic-waist pants that I could continue to wear even after I was well again. I made certain that I found pants I really liked. I write more details about simplifying our possessions in Chapter Nine.

At this time, I'm able to work two days a week and make enough money to pay my expenses. I am past my legal retirement age, so I gave myself permission to work fewer days until I'm 70 years old and I retire fully. I also saved some money as a safety net. Lately, the cost of living has increased dramatically, so I try to be a bit more careful with my grocery spending. I do plan to retire at the end of this year (2025). This does not mean that I will not work for money doing things that I enjoy, but I do not want to *have* to work to meet my financial responsibilities. We cannot know everything that may come up with our financial needs, but being on top of it allows us to have the ability to make choices. Knowing the truth about my financial situation helps me feel confident that I can make adjustments that work for me.

WORKSHEET THREE
Financial Information

I created this worksheet to help people who are interested in living their "best" lives. Another way to put it: I want to help people explore how they can create a life that works for them. A life with balance where one works, plays, and tends to self-care. In the past, when I met people who were working 60+ hours a week at a job they did not always enjoy, and they had a lack of time to do self-care, spend time with people they love, and do fun activities, I could see that it was hurting them in ways that could eventually lead to *dis-ease* of mind, body, and soul.

I have created a list of expenses below so you can reflect on your own life and create an accurate list with all *your* expenses. Everything you spend money on should be on this list. In creating your list, you may discover that you are spending money on things that you no longer want or need. You may have new expenses that you want to add to your list. Take quality time and create a very accurate list of all the items and services that you spend money on in the course of a year. We are looking at a monthly picture of your expenses, so if the cost is annual, divide it by 12 to find the monthly amount of that expense. If you are having difficulty remembering what you spent on different items, go through one month of your debit card or credit card statements or receipts of items you purchased (try to keep copies of your receipts for everything you buy if you don't use a debit or credit card to pay for things). The next list you will be looking at is your income. Reflect on all the possible income you receive in a year's time. Divide the yearly amount by 12 to get your monthly income.

Monthly Expenses

Add the dollar amount after each item below. If it is yearly, divide it by 12 months. You may want to use your journal to list your expenses and then add them up. Use a pencil.

- Housing (rent or mortgage with taxes and insurance)—

- Utilities (electricity, heating fuel [oil/propane/natural gas], internet, cable, water/sewer)—

- Phone—

- Auto expenses (loan, insurance, upkeep, yearly excise tax & registration, inspection sticker, gasoline)—

- Food (weekly food purchases as well as restaurant meals and trips to coffee shops)—

- Toiletries (personal items) and household supplies (cleaning products and paper goods)—

- Credit card(s) payments—

- Educational loans, workshops, and books—

- Recreational (streaming services, movies, concerts, gym, yoga, etc.)—

- Health insurance and medication—

- Pet expenses (food, veterinarian, other expenses)—

- Websites and domains—

- Vacation(s)—

- Doctor(s) visits, dentist, eye exams and eye wear, lab work, mental health therapy—

- Haircuts and other hair care costs—

- AAA membership and other memberships—

- Postage and office supplies (printer and copier ink), paper, envelopes, pens, pencils, staples, clips)—

- Electronic purchases and maintenance (phone, computer/laptop, printer)—

- Clothing—

- Donations—

- Hobbies—

- Other expenses (gifts, greeting cards, etc.)—

- Savings, IRA, and/or other investment contributions—

Total Monthly Expenses (any outgoing money) on a monthly basis =

Monthly Income (you may have a yearly income so divide it by 12)

- Income from working—

- Income from investments—

- Retirement income—

- Any other income—

Total Monthly Income (any incoming money) on a monthly basis =

Is my budget balanced, or do I need to adjust it?

After you compare your total expenses to your total income, you will know if you need to adjust anything to balance the money going out with the money coming in. When we see the numbers on paper, it helps us understand where our money is going. Then we can consciously

34

make changes or keep it the same. We are working with the reality of our finances.

Questions to ask yourself: Do I need to work more, or can I work less? Or do I want to continue the way it is? If I'm retired, do I need to cut my expenses, or is everything balanced?

If we realize that we make more money than we need to support ourselves, we can work less and make room to do other things that bring us joy, as well as tending to our self-care. Other times when doing this exercise, we may realize that we need to make more money to pay off loans and/or credit cards. We may get a temporary part-time job in addition to working full-time. We can also make changes in how much money we spend in different areas of our budget. We can increase some and decrease others or simply cut down on spending as much as we can and continue to have quality of life with less spending. One important point is that we should always pay off our credit card amounts every month to avoid interest fees. If you can't afford to buy a product and pay it off when your credit card bill comes in, wait (if you can) to purchase the item at a later date, when you do have the money to pay off the credit card when it's due. Also, getting credit cards with cash-back deals can be helpful in boosting your ability to save a lot of money on things you need or want.

Create your dream budget and income

I invite you to create your dream budget as well as your dream income below. Sometimes when we allow ourselves to think outside the box, we can imagine wonderful things, and in doing so we invite/attract into our lives new ways of thinking and being. If you need more writing space use a separate piece of paper or your journal. Ideas on thinking outside your box might include self-employment doing something you've always dreamed of… In the columns on the next page, list your dream budget and your dream income.

My dream budget (expenses)

My dream income

36

CHAPTER FOUR

My Use of Time

Time is one of our greatest resources because we only have so much of it, there is an expiration date and then we leave this planet.

Living a Simple Slow Pace Life Encourages Peaceful Living
We are trained at a young age to be productive if we want to be successful.
Letting go of this false belief is difficult if we are not aware that we have it.
Living a balanced life is how we reach success.
When we live a balanced life, we are able to live simply with a pace that allows us peace.

Time is one of our most valued resources and it is limited, so if we waste our time doing things we do not enjoy, we can never get it back. The way we utilize our time, as well as the pace at which we go about living our lives, heavily influences the way we experience simplicity in our daily living. The pace of life we choose is a very important factor in how we take care of ourselves. I know that I need a slow pace to my life, and when I feel forced to live life too fast, for whatever reasons, I feel annoyed, stressed, and anxious. I'm usually not very nice to be with when I experience these negative feelings. Going about life at a faster pace than is comfortable is not healthy and may cause a variety of hurtful conditions emotionally, physically, and spiritually. There is no formula or "correct" pace that one has to adopt—we each need to find our own comfort pace.

From a very young age, society encourages us to live and

work at a very fast pace. People usually feel more valued when they can multitask and get as much done in a day as possible. Sometimes people are expected to do more than is humanly possible, and this pressure may even be self-imposed. When these people can't meet the mark, they often feel they have failed. So, finding your comfortable pace and being willing to accept it is very important to your physical and mental health. Accepting the pace that fits who you are and what you can comfortably tolerate is a success and not a failure—it is a gift to yourself. If you are not retired and still working out in the field, finding the right job that allows you to work at your most comfortable pace is important. Working at a position that requires more than you can possibly accomplish is abusive.

When we are in the workforce, we spend many hours a day working. Some people have careers and other people work at jobs that hopefully fulfills them and pays a living wage. Most people need to make a living, and the trick is to find the position/job that best "fits" who you are. The secret is to find a place of employment where you feel respected and valued both as a person and as a professional/talented worker. If we find ourselves in a place of work that does not fit the person we are or that doesn't match our talents and interests we must find another job. Some people choose to be self-employed, and for them, this may be the best way to make a living because they set their own pace and utilize their chosen skills/talents. The hours that we work should allow us to feel satisfaction and comfort, or else we feel miserable and life is unpleasant. Therefore, we are spending our precious resource of time in a negative way and losing something that we can never get back—our limited amount of time on this planet.

When we are retired or close to retirement (working fewer hours), we may find it difficult to adjust to working less or not working at all. Remember when I mentioned what society values in a worker—to work hard and long hours? Seniors and people with disabilities who are slowing down their pace of life because they have to for their own health sometimes have difficulty because it has been so deeply ingrained in us that working hard and long hours is a virtue. Please know that it is of utmost importance that you slow down and adopt a healthy pace for yourself without guilt.

Having control over how we spend our time gives us the ability to incorporate into our lives every thing, person, and activity on our list of what we value. When we are informed in the area of our finances, we also have the freedom to make choices about how to live because we not only have control of how we want to spend our time, but we also know what we can afford. When I became aware of the status of my finances, as I mentioned in the last chapter, I worked on a plan to pay off my loans and credit cards. After my finances were simplified, I knew I could work less and still meet my financial obligations. In working fewer hours for pay, I had more time to do things I enjoy—like writing, doing art and photography, and other things that give my life meaning—as well as spending more time on self-care.

Concerning the use of our time, we are allowed to say no to requests from other people in the many areas of our lives—from expectations to participate in activities with family, to the simple invites to gatherings with friends. Remember that it is important to respect the pace at which we choose to live our lives. Sometimes being responsible for the total care of a parent or other relative may become too much, and it's important to know our limitations and learn to delegate help in these situations. There may be other family members or friends who would be happy to help us care for our loved one in need. Practicing healthy boundaries is an important skill to learn and maintain so we can avoid allowing others to take over our lives. Always remember that we have choices in the way we use our time.

Spending time with wonderful friends and supportive family members is important. We need to make the time for these connections. Volunteering is another way of connecting to others in meaningful ways. Remember to take the time, at least a few hours twice a week, to do something fun and creative that makes you happy!

When we are parents to young children, our time is taken up with child care and the many needs that young children have. This is very important work; however, we need to schedule self-care time on a regular basis for our own health. Our children grow up eventually, and our time becomes freer for us to work on having a balanced life with more ease. See Worksheet Four at the end of this chapter for more information on managing our time.

WORKSHEET FOUR
My Use of Time

The best way I have found for knowing how I spend my time is in creating a visual. I do this by making a circle and dividing it into sections. I have a circle for weekdays and one for weekends. The circle is a 24-hour period. I make the section sizes reflect how much time I spend on each particular activity. An example: I usually spend around eight hours of sleep a night, so my circle would have one-third for sleep. If I work eight hours a day, another third of my circle would be identified for work. Other activities might include:

- Spending time with friends and family

- Spending time with our partner, companion, or spouse

- Creativity and self-expression which gives you meaning in life (can include religion or spirituality as well as creating art…)

- Personal growth and/or education

- Recreational/fun time

- Health and wellness

- We already mentioned sleep time

- We already mentioned work time

Your circles should include all 8 sections. You can make four circles and fill the first one for weekdays and the second one for weekends the way your life is *now*. Then the third and fourth circles can be filled the way you want or wish your life could look like. The third and fourth circles give you information on how you would like to make changes in the way you use your time.

As I mentioned in Chapter Four, sometimes our lives are busier than we want them to be. That is to be expected. The important thing is that we don't allow our lives to be ruled by others. There may be times when we have young children or sick relatives to tend to; however, we have to be careful that in those situations we still take care of ourselves by asking for help and taking breaks—taking care of ourselves.

CHAPTER FIVE

My Thoughts

There is only one cause of unhappiness: the false beliefs you have in your head, beliefs so widespread, so commonly held, that it never occurs to you to question them. —Anthony deMillo

Thinking Adjustments

When life brings me emotional pain, I ask for a thinking adjustment.

A thinking adjustment allows me to broaden my focus and embrace who I am.

When I am able to reconnect to myself, I am also able to redefine what I just experienced.

The ultimate focus then brings me wisdom and understanding—hence a new outlook.

In my first book, when I worked on decluttering my thoughts so that I could allow myself to have more positive ways of thinking, I mentioned that I found this process one of the most difficult ones for me to work through. I believe that this process was hard for me because I had a tendency to think negatively about almost everything. My mother once told me, purely from a place of being supportive, that I should always expect the worst to happen, and if good things happened instead, then I'd be pleasantly surprised. Well, what happens when we think negatively? We attract negative things to happen! I did not know this until someone told me just about twelve years ago. I want to explain a bit more about why some of us tend to think negatively more easily than positively.

I believe that one of the reasons why decluttering our negative thinking process is difficult is because our thoughts have been formed from personal experiences ever since we were born. Therefore, it is from those thoughts that we form our perspectives about ourselves, people, and things. Then we live out our beliefs (the rules we live our lives by) from those perspectives, and our behaviors are usually affected by (and reflective of) our perspectives. When I say "beliefs," I don't necessarily mean religious beliefs but rather the "rules" we have adopted to live our lives by. Some of these thoughts/perspectives and beliefs have been ingrained in our minds for years and are still with us into our late sixties or older if we have not chosen to change them or remove them over the years. Some of these thoughts/perspectives and beliefs may no longer be working for us. Some people have never reflected on their thoughts/perspectives and beliefs to decide if they want to keep, change, or release them. Some of our thoughts/perspectives and beliefs were created through our experiences, and others were given to us by people who were our caregivers or others whom we trusted.

As you can see, our thoughts, perspectives, and beliefs about life are not easy to declutter, but it is possible to do so if we are willing to do the work. There is a deep feeling of release when we can let go of a thought, its perspective and belief that no longer work for us. Like anything worth having, this process is not easy but well worth the effort. And it is a long process that demands patience. One helpful tool that I suggest is using a journal. In your journal, you can write down a negative thought that is recurring, that comes to you regularly. After you write the negative thought (always date your journal entries), you can write a positive thought that is the total opposite of the negative one. You write this positive thought right below the negative one. An example of a negative thought could be:

"I'm constantly feeling sad when I think about my adult children never reaching out to me to spend time with me or show that they care about me and my well-being."

(Positive Thought) "I deserve to be happy in my life, so I plan my time doing things that makes me happy—like creative activities that brings me joy and spending time with friends who care about me. I have people whom I can count on when I need help. I wish my children a happy life."

The important thing to remember is that we *choose* not to give other people power over us, such as allowing others to "make" us feel badly or sad. We cannot change how people feel about us, but we can change how we feel about them. Sometimes our perception of a situation is not always accurate, so creating a positive thought is our way of changing our perception and possibly our belief concerning the situation and making it positive for us.

Another tool that I suggest when working with our negative thoughts, perspectives, and limiting beliefs are affirmations. I've mentioned using affirmations when working with our finances. Affirmations are very similar to positive thoughts, but they can be more general. Again, use your journal to write your affirmations that address your negative experiences. (For more information, see Worksheet Five at the end of this chapter.) An affirmation is a thought that says something positive about you and your situation. It is created with only positive words, and it is stated in the present tense. The affirmation or intention should **not** be worded to reflect what is happening to you right now, but rather, it should be worded to reflect what you want your situation to look like. An example of an affirmation: Feel free to reword it to fit your situation. "I am opening myself up to welcome and embrace my ability to think positively about myself, my skills, and my good decision-making abilities concerning my life."

Positive thoughts and affirmations are similar, but affirmations are more general and always created with positive wording in the present tense, as if it is happening right now.

I also suggest Energy Psychology Techniques as excellent tools to help us move on when we get stuck in emotional pain concerning life in general. See Worksheet Five at the end of this chapter for more information.

WORKSHEET FIVE
My Thoughts

As I already mentioned, I found that decluttering my thoughts from negative to positive was one of my most difficult tasks when I started to live a simple life. I write in Chapter Five my understanding of how it all works. Now I would like to share more information on a few tools.

TOOL #1

1. Get a journal and write a negative thought that you seem to think about often, a recurring thought. Always date your journal entries. Below the negative thought write a positive thought that counters all the negative wording with positive wording. Do this once a day or once a week, but try to be consistent, and if the same thought comes back, redo it as often as you need to. Use different positive words if you are using the same negative thought.

2. When dealing with perspectives, it may be helpful for you to write a few words on how your negative thought influences your perspective on your life at this time. Also, how does this negative thought and negative perspective affect your belief about this situation, person, or yourself? Write a few words on how your new positive thought influences your perspective and belief about this situation, person or yourself. These steps are helpful when you desire to do self reflection.

TOOL #2

The next tool I suggest is to write **affirmations** to counter any negative experience that causes you to have negative thoughts, perspectives, and beliefs. An affirmation is a thought that says something positive about you and your situation. It is created with only positive words, and it is stated in the present tense. The affirmation or intention should **not** be worded to reflect what is happening to you right now, but rather, it should be worded to reflect what you want your situation to look like because if you are seeking to change something, you *must* word it in the way you desire it to be and not the way it is. Wording it the way it is causes it to remain the way it is. We cannot continue to do the same thing over and over again and expect a different result, so wording our intentions/affirmations the way we desire our life to be is creating a change in the way we see our life and in turn creating the possibility of it changing. It also helps us to be more open to new solutions. Say the words and feel the emotions of your affirmation daily for as long as you need to until you see a change.

Examples of Affirmations: Reword them to fit your situation.
–I invite great abundance into my life at this moment, and I accept this great abundance, for I am deserving and am worthy of abundance concerning my finances (we can also use this affirmation for relationships, health, or any other issue we are seeking to change for the better). I welcome more than enough money (friendships, health…) to flow into my life.

–I am good and I deserve good, so I am opening myself in this moment to accept good in all areas of my life, especially in my finances (relationships, health…).

Just a word of caution: Affirmations are a great tool to utilize in changing our thoughts, perspectives, and beliefs, and we can expect new outcomes when we practice this tool. However, if you need medical help, affirmations are not a substitute for medical attention and treatment. If you are sick, seek medical professional help. As you get medical treatment from a professional, you can practice positive affirmations to help you become open to healing.

TOOL #3
I have used Energy Psychology Techniques for many years for both myself and my clients when we need to move through difficult situations and when using words to deal with the problems is not successful. Energy Psychology Techniques go deeper than words and are a great tool to help us move on when we get stuck in emotional

pain concerning life in general.

There are two of them that I use for myself and my clients. The first one is called EFT (Emotions Freedom Technique). I share three videos on how to do this technique on one of my YouTube channels. EFT is not copyrighted, so many people show videos. To see my videos, go to youtube.com/@tappingwithEFT and scroll down to "Marie Laverriere." (For some reason, my photo is not posted anymore.)

The next tool is Tapas Acupressure Technique ®. I was trained in this technique 17 years ago, and I use it often. I cannot publish videos on it because it is a registered trademark. If you are interested in experiencing TAT, find a professional trained in it, and you may find relief from emotional pain concerning an issue in your life. I do offer TAT sessions, so if you are interested, you can view my website for contact information: LivingWithSimplicity.com

CHAPTER SIX

Finding Meaning in My Life

I looked in temples, churches and mosques, but I found the Divine within my heart. —Rumi

I Am a Spiritual Being Having a Human Experience
I am constantly reminding myself who I am.
Since I was a child, I felt that I had an inner life that was as important as my outer life.
My inner life is my spirit self, and my outer life is my physical self. Both facets of me are important and influence my experience on my journey.

I will share my journey in finding meaning in my life, but my hopes are that you will all find your own ways because there are many paths to finding meaning in one's life, and they are all authentic and sacred.

For a very long time, I thought that the only way I could find meaning in my life was by engaging on a spiritual journey, and I still believe this. However, early on, I was not always certain of what that meant exactly, but I believed that one had to follow a religion and practice its doctrines and dogmas as a requirement to connect to one's spirituality. As a young adult, I discovered that some religions did not always live up to what was preached by their leaders and followers. I decided that I needed to find other ways of connecting to meaning in my life. My mother was very loyal to her religion and a very good person, and I respect people who follow their religion faithfully with kindness and love. However, my life experiences, after searching and learning about many world religions, brought me to a different path.

I guess one could say that I experienced a decluttering and simplifying when I embarked on my journey to find meaning in my life in my sixties. My old way of thinking was that there was a separation between being human and being spiritual. The idea of existing as a spiritual being having a human experience came to me when I was a young child. It was a quick moment, and then I forgot it soon after it happened. However, I remembered it again much later in my life, and it felt authentic and right. A few years passed, and I read it in a book written by a French Jesuit priest named Pierre Teilhard de Chardin. Teilhard lived between 1881 and 1955. In one of his books, he wrote, "We are not human beings having a spiritual experience. We are spiritual beings having a human experience." His statement resonated very deeply within me because it is the heart of my spiritual journey.

As spiritual beings, we are already one with God, and since God is Spirit, we are connected. All the years of being told that I needed to earn God's love and do this and that were all false. We do not need to do anything to be connected to Spirit—otherwise known as God. I'd like to define what I mean by the term "spiritual beings." Spiritual beings are nonphysical beings: One could say it is our soul or spirit within each of us. I define "human beings" as physical beings, otherwise known as people. So, for us to walk and talk and experience being on this physical planet, we have to be physical. But the real us is in spirit form. I believe that our spirit or soul is the real us—the spiritual being. Our spirit being speaks to us through our inner wisdom, also known as our intuition (our "gut feeling"). Our intuition/inner wisdom is an energetic expression of our spiritual being. Our intuition is the pure wisdom within each of us, and it is very important that we connect to it often. It would be wonderful if we could just let it flow continuously, but for some reason we don't.

The real us—spiritual being—is one with all that is, otherwise known as the Source, the Divine, or God. This is why I don't believe we have to earn God's love or do anything in particular to be connected to God because by our true nature we are one with God. The human experience that we are all having sometimes overshadows who we really are. Ways that we can allow our spirit/soul to express itself can be done at times through expressions of creativity— creating beautiful things. However, our spirit can also express itself to us through our experience in nature—a beautiful Monarch butterfly landing on our arm, or a sunrise—and capture it in our memory or with our cell phone cameras. These moments allow us to give a voice to our true selves and gives us the ability to feel the flow of passion that sustains all of life. Other ways that we can allow our spirit to express itself are through kindness, gentleness, and goodness toward people around us and even to ourselves. There are no limits to the abilities we have to let our spirit express itself and touch the world with passion, peace, and love.

One of the ways that I connect with Spirit (my spirit being and God) is that I acknowledge daily that I am thankful for everything in my life. Other ways that I connect are by doing a simple five-minute meditation, and after this meditation, I ask God for a golden nugget of wisdom for the day (I have instructions on Worksheet Six).

The photo on the book cover has four stones that I picked up on the beach across the street from my home while taking my daily walks. The stones are all natural in color, but when I stacked them and took the picture with my phone camera, I could not believe my eyes when I saw the photo because one of the stones is gold. I felt that my prayers for a golden nugget of wisdom was being validated.

In closing, I want to stress that when we create, we allow our passion to flow, and this causes our creative juices to express themselves. In doing this, we give our souls a voice on this planet. In the next chapter, I write more about creativity and the many ways in which one can express it and how it is such a wonderful way of connecting to meaning in our lives.

WORKSHEET SIX
Finding Meaning in My Life

We all find meaning in our lives in different ways. Some people follow spiritual practices like meditation, yoga, prayer, walks in nature (beach, garden, mountain, forest…). Other people utilize creative expressions such as art to feel and experience meaning in their lives. Others find religion helpful to them to connect to what feels important and gives their lives meaning. Some people offer acts of kindness to others through volunteering, and the list goes on.

It does not matter how we find meaning in our lives, but what does matter is that we are able to find ways to connect to meaning in our lives on a regular basis.

I shared with you my belief in the statement that "we are spiritual beings having a human experience," and I live my life incorporating connection to my spirit being so that I have guidance as a human person. I use a simple five-minute meditation with a cleansing breath before and after, as well as asking for my golden nugget of wisdom, as ways to help me be connected to the voice of my spirit, my intuition. Sometimes, spending time in silence to experience conscious awareness or to be in the present moment is a wonderful way to find meaning. Dancing, singing, or playing an instrument, listening to a meaningful song or a piece of music, and so many more ways…are all paths to nurture and connect to meaning in our lives.

As you can see, there are no limits to finding meaning in our lives; the only thing that may stop us is an inability to find what works for us. In this worksheet, I challenge you to start thinking about this (if you have not done so already) and write down the specific ways that you find meaning in your life and how you incorporate it in your daily living. I have listed below instructions on how to do a cleansing breath, the five-minute simple meditation, and the golden nugget of wisdom prayer as possible tools to help you if you are looking for suggestions to begin the process.

52

Cleansing Breath—

Sometimes when we are dealing with a lot of stress, the best way to calm ourselves immediately is to take a cleansing breath. This is how you do it: With your mouth closed, breathe in through your nose as far in as you can go, then breathe out of your mouth slowly and completely. Do it only once, because if you do it more than once at a time you may get lightheaded. Do this cleansing breath as often as you need to in the course of your day. Try to always breathe from your belly, as this is the best way to get the most oxygen into your system. Shallow chest breathing is not as useful.

Five-Minute Simple Meditation—

Sit comfortably in a chair with your feet flat on the floor and your back straight. Tilt your head very slightly forward and either close your eyes or keep them open and gaze at a spot on the floor. Whichever you choose, continue to do so throughout the meditation. Begin by taking a cleansing breath, ***then breathe normally throughout the meditation***. With each out-breath, count from one to ten as you breathe normally. Do four sets of these. Use your fingers to keep track from one to four sets. So, you will count *one* on your first out-breath, *two* on your second out-breath, and so on. This should take about five minutes. Don't worry if your counting goes past ten; just return to one as often as you need to. You can continue if you want to do it longer. You do this daily. When doing this simple meditation, you may feel the benefits of calm and peace. This meditation may; help you relax, ground you in your body, clear your mind, help you feel lighter within, and help you deal with stress in a refreshed way. It can also help you feel the connection with your spirit/soul. Try to find the same time every day to do this, so it can become a regular practice/a habit.

Golden Nuggets of Wisdom—

1. I do the simple five-minute meditation.
2. I do a cleansing breath.
3. I ask God/Spirit for a golden nugget of wisdom that may be helpful for me today.
4. I listen with my heart, and work hard at keeping myself out of my head/thoughts.
5. I say my name three times and speak whatever words flow out of my mouth.

Another way of receiving the golden nugget is by writing the message that comes to me as I stay out of my own thinking.

6. When a thought comes out of nowhere (not from my own mind), I listen. This is the golden nugget. Most of the time, after the message stops, I write it in my journal so I won't forget it. I've received many wise thoughts from practicing this "prayer." You can also substitute asking the Universe or asking your inner wisdom/intuition for "asking God." This exercise has been helpful to me for over 20 years. Some wisdom I've received has been very helpful to me, and I had never thought of it before. Other times, the wisdom is familiar because I may have received it before but have forgotten it and I really need to listen to it and follow it.

Feel free to develop your own form of prayer or meditation. I share these because they work for me but it's important for you to find what works for you.

CHAPTER SEVEN

Creativity—How Do I Allow My Passion to Flow?

Whatever feeds your spirit, makes your heart sing, and fuels your passion, you must do it!

Finding and Expressing Our Creativity

When I express my creativity, I give voice to my soul.
I allow my passion to flow, and my purpose evolves.
Expressing our own personal creativity is as important as eating and breathing.
Finding our path to being creative and living it, is an extremely important expression of ourselves.

I believe that being creative is as important to our health and life as water and food, and there are innumerable ways that one can create—cooking a meal, baking, creating our living spaces, choosing our clothing in the morning, knitting, painting, photography, etc. We have so many opportunities. People who create have a connection to their true selves, while people who don't create miss out on this connection and may be starving the expressions of their souls. I've met many people who say, "I'm not an artist," and I say, "We are all artists; we just have to find our medium—the kind of expression that fits us." Creating is an active expression, while reading a book or watching a movie is a passive experience, not a creative activity. A creative activity or expression may cause our passion to flow and bring us joy. For me, writing is one of my creative expressions, and when I engage in this activity, I feel that there is a part of me that is able to feel passion in words and thoughts and it's exciting. Another way that I am able to be creative is with photography. Almost everyone on this planet has a cell phone with a camera in it, ready to capture a moment of beauty in nature or some other source of inspiration.

If you have not participated in being creative, I suggest exploring different activities so you can find the ones that best fit your tastes and abilities and allow your passion to flow. As I already mentioned, some people find their passion in cooking/baking a variety of foods, and this is their creative expression. Other people paint pictures of nature, people, or objects, and this is their way of allowing their passion to flow. Gardening, sewing, knitting, woodworking, and numerous other activities can be a person's way of expressing their creativity.

Sometimes when people are depressed they find it difficult to motivate themselves to find and participate in a creative expression. But there are easy things we can do to get started. One idea is a mandala coloring book that we can purchase; Amazon sells them, as do most bookstores. Some have easy patterns and others have more complex ones—you choose. Mandalas are circular designs, and some people feel that coloring them helps calm them and give them a peaceful feeling. I suggest also purchasing fine-tip colored markers, which are available in sets of 12 or more assorted colors. Coloring mandalas with fine-tip markers is a way to start energizing your creative juices. Choose the colors that help you feel good, and fill in the mandala design. When finished, you can put it on a wall in your home and see the effects of the design and colors on your mood.

Another way of starting to motivate yourself to be creative is to be present when you are in or near nature. When you see something enticing, take a photo of it with your cell phone camera. I once saw three chipmunks sitting on top of a large fencepost. They stayed put in their poses as I took several photos. If I had not been present in that moment of my life, at that specific time, I would never had noticed them. This photo makes me laugh every time I see it because the chipmunks were acting like statues and not moving, perhaps thinking I would not see them.

Creating is part of our soul's purpose in being alive in this human experience. When we create, we give our souls a voice on this planet. Some people take art classes offered at adult education programs or online. If you are not sure what type of fine art you are attracted to, visit your local library or go online and view art books of different types and you may get inspired. I enjoy walking through an art store and examining all the art supplies for inspiration on starting a project. I'm mostly attracted to calligraphy and acrylic paint materials. I took a few years of calligraphy classes, and I enjoy this art form. I usually embellish my calligraphy with acrylic paints to give them color and form. You do not need to create fine art to be creative; check out the list of ideas on Worksheet Seven to get your interest going.

And seriously, it is really important for you to find your creative expressions and do them on a regular basis. It's best to have a routine of specific days and times so that it becomes a habit and you can maintain this powerful way of giving your life meaning and joy.

WORKSHEET SEVEN
Ideas for Creative Expressions

Participating in creative activities is such a broad topic, I could write an entire book on ideas and ways to express one's creativity. Simply put, creative expressions are any activities we do that cause us to create something. It can be as simple as choosing our clothing in the morning as we match and accessorize our outfit. It can be a bit more complex, like cooking and baking or redecorating our living or working spaces. When we create, our passion flows, and we usually feel excited and happy. Just don't choose something that you don't enjoy doing.

As I have mentioned before, I believe that creating is part of your soul's expression in being alive in this human experience. It is definitely a way for us to allow our souls to have a voice in this world. I have listed below a variety of creative activities, and I am certain that you can add to this list from your own experiences. What is most important is that you find your creative expression, and you create at least once a week if not more often. It works best if you have a regular day(s) and time(s) every week so that it becomes a habit. In Chapter Seven, I suggested an easy activity to get you started if you find it difficult to get started—coloring a mandala with fine-tip markers. It's also helpful if you find a space in your home dedicated to creating so that you don't need to get the supplies and clear out a space every time you want to create.

Photography

Calligraphy

Drawing and/or painting

Sculpture

Pottery

Writing (poems, articles, stories, or even a book…)

Baking

Cooking

Gardening

Collage

Decluttering a room and organizing it perfectly

Playing a musical instrument

Singing

Creating a song (music and/or words)

Designing clothing

Knitting, embroidery, crocheting, sewing

Interior designing

And so many more…

CHAPTER EIGHT

My Health and the Importance of Caring for Myself

As an adult, I am the only person who is responsible for my health. If I fail to honor myself with my best efforts to having a healthy body, mind, and soul, then I may suffer the negative consequences.

When we are young, we don't think much about our health, but as we grow older, our physical health demands more attention and care. Another aspect of health is our mental health. There are many studies in the United States confirming that numerous people suffer from anxiety and depression. I remember working at a social service agency in New Mexico where I was a supervisor to eight caseworkers. The pressure that my supervisor and her supervisor were placing on my workers was inhumane. There was no way that these workers could accomplish what they were told was expected of them. I remember telling them of the added expectations with an apology, every time a new directive was created. I knew that their time was already more than full, so I simply asked them to do their best at their jobs. This same agency would hire professional trainers once or twice a year for one-day workshops to help the workers deal with anxiety in their lives. Why did they cause their workers to have anxiety in the first place? I found this management style very dysfunctional.

I believe that we are all responsible for our own well-being, physically, emotionally, and spiritually. When we go about our lives with the intention of balance and healthy living, we seem to attract opportunities to live this way. Let me start with our need to work, to make a living.

Many people think they have to accept work that comes along

without much reflection on how it will affect them health-wise. Yes, most of us need to work to make a living, but let us not forget that we can make choices that are in our best interest. There are many people who enjoy their jobs and are happy, but there are many other people on this planet who work very hard at their paying jobs and suffer greatly because their jobs are not a good fit for them. I remember once applying for a professional LCSW position in a school district. At my interview, when I listened to the person who would have been my boss and heard all of her expectations of the person she was looking to hire, I thought, *there is no way that I will accept this position.* She verbally listed work that would have taken three people to accomplish. When we apply for work, it's not only the employer who decides if we are "good enough" or the "right person for the job"; it is also our evaluation of the employer and whether the job is the right fit for us—do we agree with their policies? Remember, we always have choices, and sometimes another job or self-employment is a better choice for us.

Studies show that Americans are not the healthiest people in the world. Many of us do not eat healthy food, get enough quality sleep, or exercise as we should (a 20-30 minute brisk daily walk is a very good start). It is also important (as I mentioned already) that we work in positions where we feel comfortable, appreciated, and fulfilled, with reasonable hours and a fair and livable wage. Taking time to experience fun activities on a regular basis is also important. Simplifying our time after we have the knowledge of our finances and know how many hours we need to work to pay our bills and live comfortably is very important for self-care. It allows us choices in the way we live.

Review the list you made in Chapter Two on the things, people, and activities you value in your life. This is a roadmap to the kind of work you might want to explore. The activities list leads us to contemplate and make decisions on the work we want to spend our lives doing that will bring us the most joy. The list also tells us what we value in things and people who make us happy. Being healthy is a responsibility that we all have throughout our adult lives. When we are young children, it's our caregivers' responsibility to help us be healthy, but when we are young adults and older, the responsibility is ours.

To summarize the different factors in healthy living:

1. Manage our use of **time** as well as our pace of comfort.
2. Eat **healthy food** (always good-tasting, of course).
3. **Exercise** daily (a 20–30 minute walk is a good way to begin to exercise).
4. Get enough daily **quality sleep** so we can function comfortably during the day.
5. **Work** that complements our skills and interests and pays us a living wage.
6. **Taking time to be with people who love us** and appreciate who we are.
7. **Make time to play.**
8. Make the time to find activities for **self-development**.
9. Make the time to do **creative expressions** and **find meaning** in our lives.

Each of these areas must be tended to if we want to be truly healthy. Being healthy is a lot of work, and it brings our lives a quality that is beyond fulfilling, and when we neglect this very important responsibility, we suffer greatly.

The nine categories listed above are important to reflect on and evaluate as to how well we are meeting our needs in these different areas. I suggest that you write down the categories in your journal, and then write how you are addressing each of them at this time in your life. To end this activity, you can then write a paragraph below each category with the possible changes or improvements you can make to experience better mental and physical health, always keeping in mind how to accomplish good health in the context of living a simple life.

WORKSHEET EIGHT
My Health and Ways to Tend to Myself

In Chapter Eight, I have suggested several ideas for tending to one's well-being. I have added more information in this worksheet concerning other points of interest that may be helpful to you when working on being healthy.

Ways to Help Heal and Raise One's Self-Esteem and Confidence

Many of us struggle with not having good self-esteem. When our self-esteem is healthy, we believe in ourselves, we trust our judgment, and we can depend on our inner wisdom to sustain us in good and bad times. When our self-esteem is not healthy we doubt ourselves in every way. We depend on others to tell us what to do, how to do it, what to think, and we are dependent on other people to help us feel good about ourselves. Self-esteem is the doorway to our intuition, so when we have low self-esteem, we have difficulty connecting with our gut feelings.There are ways that we can nurture our self-esteem, and here are a few suggestions:

1. Start to **create a grateful journal or add to it if you already have one.** Always write the date with each entry. Re-read your grateful journal weekly so that you remember all the good things in your life. The little things and the big things. And remember that you deserve all these good things. You are worthy of all these wonderful things in your life.

2. Write **affirmations** concerning all the places in your life that you feel you need a more positive outlook. See information on how to create affirmations on Worksheet Five. Work on all your feelings of inadequacy by creating an affirmation to counter each of them.

3. Create. Choose to create the kind of "art" that you enjoy working with. We are all artists, and we just have to figure out what our creative expression is. Photography, poetry, painting, drawing, landscaping, interior decorating, playing an instrument and/or writing music, designing and/or creating clothing, gardening, writing essays or a book, baking, cooking, or whatever your heart desires—just create. Human beings need to create as much as they need to care for their bodies. When we are able to express our creativity, our self-esteem is nurtured. Do not be a perfectionist—just create. Make the time for it. If you can't figure out what kind of art to do, purchase some art supplies and try them out. See adult education offerings and other community classes. Also, check out YouTube for exposure to a variety of approaches for creative opportunities. Remember, creating includes more than just doing "art." See Worksheet Seven for more ideas.

4. Honor yourself. I believe that honoring ourselves is the first step in loving ourselves. Be kind to yourself. Do nice things for yourself. Go through your list of **what you value (things, people, and activities)** and make certain you have made room to include those things, people, and activities in your life. Hang out with people who love you and treat you well. Break ties with people who mistreat you and make you feel bad. If you start being more positive with yourself, you will start being more positive with others, and therefore, you'll attract positive people into your life.

5. Make a list of what soothes you. Make the time to do some of these things every day. We all have ways to soothe ourselves. My way is to spend some time rocking in a rocking chair. Human beings have a need to soothe themselves on a regular basis. When we experience stress and anxiety, the only way we can find relief is to put into practice simple experiences of soothing and calming. Below I provide a list of ideas that might work for you, and I invite you to add your own.

-Swing, glide, or use a hammock.
-Walk on the beach, in the woods, or in a garden and listen to the sounds of nature.
-Listen to calming music.
-Wrap yourself tightly in a blanket.

-Have a cup of warm, non-caffeinated tea or other warm beverage.

-Suck on a sour lollipop.

-Chew gum.

-Do the five-minute meditation.

-Take a cleansing breath.

-Listen to a guided imagery.

-Take a warm/hot shower or bath.

-Sit outside in the sun and check in with your five senses.

-Walk briskly around the block or down the street.

-Think about your favorite place on the planet and imagine being there; remember the joy and fun you had, and imagine that you are experiencing it all over again.

-Make a list of everything that you are grateful for or read your grateful journal.

-Wear comfortable clothing.

-Pat a dog or a cat.

-Read a "feel-good" book or watch a "feel-good" movie.

-Smell orange essential oil right from the bottle.

-Rub a smooth stone with your thumb and forefinger.

-Rub your favorite scented lotion all over your body.

-Surround yourself with art that feeds your soul.

6. Don't just fit in—be yourself! Show up in life as who you are! Remember that your self-worth depends on you and not what others say about you. I have a theory that most people see us through their own personal life lenses, and they don't really see us; therefore, their opinions of us are distorted by their own views of themselves.

7. Get an empty journal or use a computer and start to **write a reflection on the last 30 years of your life** concerning life lessons that you experienced. These life lessons may have come from difficult life events, but if you frame them as learning opportunities, you can benefit by recalling them because life lessons are blessings that you have received through your many life experiences. If you are younger, this reflection will cover less time, and if you are older, it may encompass 30+ or more years. Some people use a timeline to help them remember the highlights of their life and better recall what happened and when. Write about detailed experiences and what you learned about yourself, life, and the world. At the end of the reflection, you can write yourself a short letter thanking yourself for all you went through and congratulating yourself for doing this great work in your life.

Ideas on Self-Care Relaxation

The Cleansing Breath and the Five-Minute Simple Meditation is found on Worksheet Six. Both of these tools are great for self care and relaxation.

Listen to a Guided Imagery

Find guided imageries that fit your style. I found one on YouTube. You can check it out by typing exactly "15-minute guided meditation & visualization/fear & anxiety release." There is a woman from Dublin sitting in front of a colorful tree. Her voice is very relaxing, and she walks you through a calming and relaxing journey. There are several other selections on that site, or you can find an app that offers guided imageries.

Check In with Your Five Senses

This activity is more effective if you can do it outside, maybe on your back porch. You begin by taking a Cleansing Breath then you ask yourself what you hear and you listen to everything you hear and name each thing. You go on to ask what you see and do the same, naming everything one at a time. The next question is what do you smell? Say everything you smell. What taste do you have in your mouth is the next question. Maybe you just had coffee or some other food item. Name the taste in your mouth. The last sense you check in with is what you feel. How does your face feel? your skin? your head? Perhaps the sun is shining on you, and you feel the warmth of the sun, or there is a cool breeze and you feel that. Be as thorough as you can, and when you're finished you may feel more grounded in your body, clearer in your mind, and perhaps even more peaceful.

Grateful Journal

I've mentioned keeping a grateful journal already, but I thought I'd mention it again. You can purchase a nice journal and enter everything that you can remember being grateful for. Date every entry. Write in it when you remember a new grateful thought. Having a grateful journal is important because there are times that we forget the things, people, and events that we are grateful for in our lives, and having a journal to remind us is a great tool. When we are having a bad day, looking into our grateful journal can be very soothing. As we get older our sense of being grateful becomes more inclusive of basic things like "I'm able to walk today without pain" and things like that—things that we take for granted when we are younger.

Journaling

Journaling is a great way for people to process their life experiences. You can journal daily or weekly or even just when you feel like it. Don't make this activity a burden for yourself. You may choose to write only once a year or several times a month. It's all up to you how often you journal. The role of journaling is to try to capture any lesson that you feel you have learned so that you won't forget it. Dating each entry is also important so you can see your progress as time moves on.

CHAPTER NINE

How to Move Forward?

You know you are living a simple life when you have the freedom to make choices that allows you to live your life with peace and happiness.

Have you ever asked yourself what a simple life means to you? What would your life look like if you could create it to be more simple? If you are desiring a simple life with opportunities to experience more peace, relaxation, and the things you love to do, what changes would you have to implement to make this happen? Does simplifying your life mean fewer possessions? Fewer time commitments? Less thinking and more positive thoughts? Everyone has the ability to create their own customized simple life. Remember that it's a process and cannot be done all at once. It's important to start to think about it and put some of your thoughts in writing as you create a plan to start the process. Answering the questions in this paragraph may be helpful for you to better define how you want your life to be.

Living with simplicity looks different for everyone because the process and the outcome are very personal. In doing this work, we have to include our unique desires and needs as well as our tastes and the personal experiences that have made us the person we are today. When I think back to my childhood, I remember the urge I had to keep my life as simple as I could. It was the way we lived as a family. Five years ago, when my friend invited me to consider living in one of his tiny cottages, seeing the cottage that I now live in was surreal for me. The memory of my childhood cottage came right back to me. I believe that I always had a deep desire to live a very simple life. As I grew up and did what most people do, like getting married and having children, I somehow lost my way with living a simple life. Some people do live a simple life married with children, but for some reason, the desire I'd once had totally disappeared. My friend was the source or impetus that helped me get back to my true self, and I am forever grateful.

I have outlined instructions on how to get started and move through living with simplicity. Let us begin:

- Start with rereading the first paragraph of this chapter, and in your journal answer the questions as truthfully as you can. Take your time so that you can be honest and thorough.

- Human beings need motivation to accomplish changes in their lives. So, identify the motivation that you need to want to live a more simple life.

- The process of simplifying our lives includes decluttering. In fact, most people begin to simplify their lives by decluttering their possessions. When we start to declutter and keep what we need and want, the desire to buy more things pretty much stops because we know we have everything we need. In my case, living in a small space is a very good deterrent to buying things I don't need—I just don't have the space for more things.

- Organizing our things and other facets of our lives is not the same as decluttering. We can rearrange and move things around, and I call this organizing, which is a good thing to do after we declutter. To **declutter** means we clear space, and we are willing to get rid of things we no longer use or need. Sometimes this allows us to make room for new items that serve us better. An example would be for me to declutter my many pots and pans of different sizes and replace them with a simple set of fewer pieces that I find myself using regularly.

- Living with simplicity means to maintain living with only the things we need and use; it's a way of life. We can keep things that we love to have: An example for me is that I enjoy having crystal pieces of different types. I appreciate their beauty, and I keep them on my bookshelf with a candle and a few other items that make me feel good whenever I glance at them. I don't feel the urge to buy more of them; I simply enjoy the ones I have. Before I moved into my small cottage, I eliminated 95 percent of my possessions because I did not need all that stuff, nor could I fit all of it in the small space I was moving into. I will describe the different areas to declutter as I continue this chapter, beginning with our clothing.

1. As I mentioned before, a good place to start to **declutter** is with our **clothing**. I suggest that you create a list of the pieces of clothing that you need to have to live your life comfortably for work, casual, and formal wear. This is how I did it: After I created my list, I placed all my clothing on my bed, emptied all closets and drawers. I then placed a full-length mirror in front of me and tried on every single piece of clothing that I thought I might want to keep. This process helped me to keep only what I needed and would wear. I chose clothing in colors that looked good on me, felt good on me as far as the texture of the fabric, and it had to fit me—be the right size. Some people feel bad about getting rid of clothing that they paid a lot of money for, but I say do not keep anything for any reason other than you need it, it fits, and you will use it because you like it. I had plastic bins of clothing that were too small, which I kept in case I lost weight, and too big in case I gained weight. I got rid of all these bins. After I was done and had a pile of clothing that passed all the points above, I decided how many pieces I would keep according to the list I'd created before going through the clothing and gave away the rest.

      I always found it complicated with a touch of anxiety to think about what to wear every day so I did something to change that. I call this living with simplicity with my clothing. I found comfortable clothing (some I already had and some I bought) with the colors that I feel look good on me, and of course I want the clothing to fit me well. My winter clothing consists of regular long pants (some blue jeans and some black pants) and shirts with three-quarter sleeves (I have a few long-sleeved turtlenecks for really cold weather); some are black and some are blue. I then did the same with summer clothing, except the pants are short and the shirts are sleeveless. I mostly wear similar outfits because I found the perfect fitting fabrics, and now I don't think about what to wear—I just wear pretty much the same from day to day. This has eliminated the time I would spend to figure out what to wear. I do the same with my jewelry. I make my own jewelry, and I have a small box with simple pendants, bracelets, and earrings. They match the clothing I wear, and again I don't have to fuss over what to wear— it's all so very simple. The way I just described my wardrobe works for me in living a simplified life, but another person might find a different way to create their wardrobe, and this is what I mean when I say that living a simple life is custom to everyone. We all do it differently, and it's all perfectly acceptable.

To simplify one's life is to make it uncomplicated in as many ways as possible. As I have already written, people can live in larger homes and still live simple lives because it's not the size of the home that determines living with simplicity, but rather the *manner* in which we live our lives. My decision to live in a tiny home 100 steps from the ocean was my main motivation to begin to live with simplicity. Even though I was motivated, the process was not easy, and I did go through all my possessions three times. I mentioned before that I used the mantra, "If I haven't used this in the past year, I don't need it." I had a few months to purge and pack before moving. Decluttering is a process, so don't think you can do it quickly and by going through your possessions only once. Also, sentimental items that you will never use can be photographed and then discarded. You still have the memory, and you can view your photographs if you want to see it again. Another way to preserve something sentimental like grandmother's set of china, that you never use, is to keep a cup and saucer and give the rest of it away. I will outline ways of simplifying other aspects of one's possessions as I move forward in this chapter. I will do this to help the readers who have not read my first book.

2. Medicine cabinet—Go through the cabinet and ask yourself if you still need each of these products, and also check the expiration dates. You will be surprised as to how many items have expired. Prescription medication as well as vitamins and supplements are usually found in the medicine cabinet as well as Band-Aids and similar items.

 3. **Toiletries**—Shampoo, hair conditioner, body soap, facial cleanser, deodorant, body lotion, hair gel, face moisturizer, toothbrush, toothpaste, mouth rinse, mouthwash, floss, and basic makeup items (makeup also has an expiration date). Throw away all the items you do not use. Again, we may have bought expensive makeup and did not like it but felt guilty so we kept it—it's time to toss it in the trash! Eventually you will find your favorite products for each of the items above and your life will be more simple.

4. **Household cleaning supplies**—I use a broom, a dustpan and brush, a sponge mop, a vacuum cleaner (I found a rechargeable one that stores easily and takes hardly any space), and a duster on a stick. For cleaning "soaps" I use Windex, Comet, Meyers multipurpose spray, and Pine-Sol liquid to wash the floors or for other heavy-duty cleaning. I use dish soap and hand soap, and I buy a larger bottle of each and smaller bottles that I refill. I keep the smaller bottles on the sink to use regularly—one hand soap small bottle on the bathroom sink, and one of each (hand and dish soap) on the kitchen sink. I also have a sponge that I keep in a suction-cupped stainless holder in the sink to wash the dishes. You have to find the cleaning supplies that you enjoy using, but don't duplicate and have three types of soap for one purpose because that can be a waste of space and money.

5. **Food**—Again, my reference is from living in a tiny space, so my food cupboards are limited even though I find them quite adequate. I go through my food shelves/cupboards every so often because things expire. Also, before I go food shopping (weekly), I research what I already have as I make my list for the following week's meals. I have a spice rack on my kitchen wall that is easy to see and find things in. The main food shelving unit is located on top of the stove and refrigerator. There are two shelves measuring 4'6" long by 12" deep with doors.

I have smaller tray-like containers that I put jars and boxes in so I can reach them and keep tabs on what I have in there. I also have two narrow shelves to the right of the refrigerator where I keep my bottled water and other cooking ingredients. Checking what I need before going food shopping saves me a lot of money. And the fact that my refrigerator/freezer are smaller than an average one helps me not to waste food because I only buy what I can use in one to two weeks' time.

6. Pots, pans, cookware, dishes, bowls, cups, glasses, utensils, and silverware—I have dinner with a friend daily, so I keep four plates, cups, bowls, and so on. I've shrunk down the number of my pots and pans as I go from year to year and notice what I don't need or use. My cabinet under the sink in the kitchen is where I have space for all my pots, pans, cookware, pie plates, bread tins, square metal cooking pans, and so on. My cleaning products are stored there as well as in the closet under my bathroom sink. I have a blender, a small food processor, a toaster, a waffle maker, and a handheld mixer. I keep my dishes, cups, and glasses in my shelving unit in the kitchen area.

7. Books—I had a deep love for books for many years, and I think at one time I had close to 3,000 books. When I moved into this cottage, I could only keep about 90 books: At the time, the shelf over my Murphy bed was the only place I had room for books. Getting rid of books was very difficult for me, but my motivation for living in this tiny cottage helped me sort through them.

8. Paperwork—We all have important information that we need to keep, either to refer to or simply to have when we need it. I had two deep four-drawer metal filing cabinets full of paperwork before I moved into the cottage. I spent eight hours going through everything and filling several large green contractor bags to throw away. I was lucky to find a deep, almost-new two-drawer metal filing cabinet (at the location where I donated most of my unneeded possessions), and I made it work. Everything fits in there, and at least once a year, I go through it and purge what I no longer need. My paperwork is in manila folders in alphabetical order.

9. Office supplies, sewing kit, art supplies—Jewelry-making beads and supplies and several other items that I keep in baskets and decorative boxes are now stored in shelving units with doors. I've gone through all these separate items at least twice a year for the last five years to maintain decluttering. I will continue to do this because as human beings we accumulate things, sometimes without realizing it.

10. Shoes, slippers, sandals, sneakers—I used to keep these behind the bathroom door in a plastic shoe rack, but now I have space to put all eleven pairs on a shelf in one of my large cabinets with doors. I have a rubber mat on top of one of my cabinets where I keep my three pairs of winter boots during the time I use them.

11. Wall hangings and other knickknacks—I chose the pieces that I hang on my walls very carefully. I have to really love it because my wall space is limited. I also have crystal pieces and a few other things that have meaning for me (I mentioned this earlier), and they are placed on a portion of my shelf where I keep my 60 books (yes, I am still downsizing my books) and a few baskets. I have the philosophy that less is more. I don't like the "clutter look," so I avoid having too many knickknacks and wall hangings.

12. Trash cans—I have a trash can in both the bathroom and the kitchen. Both are new and smaller. The kitchen one is narrow and fits in a specific place. The bathroom one is also very small because I added an apartment-size washer/dryer in the bathroom this year.

13. Work space—Recently, I decided to create a permanent work space (as I mentioned earlier). I bought a 39"-high workbench (metal legs and wooden top) and a stool so I now have a place to work and do my different art projects. It took me five years to figure out how I could best use the tiny space in my cottage for work.

14. Rugs—I bought an area rug for the living room, a new runner rug for in front of the kitchen sink, and a smaller rug for in front of the bathroom sink. It makes the space look cozy, and the dog loves to lie on them.

15. Lighting—I had many floor lamps when I lived in my apartment by the river, and a few of them had mica shades, which I felt made the room feel calm. Floor space is so limited in my cottage that I gave away all my floor lamps and now have four wall lights—the kind that swing out. I found mica-colored light bulbs that I put in two of the lights, and the other two lights have regular bulbs. I keep my Tiffany-style lamp on my kitchen table. It's just the right size, and I enjoy the bright colors it has when it's turned on.

16. Washer/dryer—One thing I had to adjust to was not having my own washer/dryer in my home. There are two sets of washer/dryers on the premises (shared by all 10 cottages), just a few steps from my cottage, but there is nothing as convenient as having my own machines. My friend installed a new apartment-size combo washer/ dryer in my bathroom for Christmas this past year. He moved the toilet sideways to make room for this machine, and it all fits perfectly. I now have my own washer/dryer, and I *really* appreciate it!

17. Screened Porch Area—To make my cottage my "perfect" home, I need a screened area so I can sit outside. I'm not certain how that will work, but it will happen sometime this coming spring because the mosquitos and ticks are very bad in this neck of the woods.

18. Furniture—My basic furniture pieces are a kitchen table with two chairs, a stove and refrigerator, three big shelving units with doors, two rocker/recliner stuffed chairs, a bed (I eliminated the Murphy bed and got an extra-long twin bed with a headboard and electric frame). Before and after I had shoulder surgery, I just could not handle moving the Murphy bed up and down anymore. I also have a workbench with a stool, a very thin foldable treadmill (it leans up against the wall when not in use), a two-drawer filling cabinet, two wall-mounted 6.5' shelves, a small side table, and two folding TV trays. I have a 20" shelf that holds a basket and has hooks underneath for coats and jackets near the door of the cottage. On my front porch, I have a small Weber grill and an all-weather white rocking chair. My five windows (including the door) all have blinds for privacy.

These are all my furnishings. I live alone with my dog, Henry, and it all works. The cottage has a cathedral ceiling that adds a feeling of space. I don't think I would feel comfortable without the cathedral ceiling. The cottage would feel smaller.

This chapter is a simple walk-through on how one can start to declutter one's possessions. After our living space is decluttered and organized, we may be ready to start simplifying other areas in our lives if we have not already begun to do so. I have outlined in Chapters One through Eight, areas I found important to simplify in my own life. I have a worksheet after each of these eight chapters if you feel you need a little more guidance.

If you are interested in viewing a short video of a tour of my tiny cottage you can go to (YouTube.com/@livingasimplelife) and see video 87, I will be posting it at the end of June 2025.

CHAPTER TEN

Living a Simplified Life as Seniors

Twists & Turns
Life sure has a way of throwing us curveballs.
I have had my share, and when I reflect on my journey,
I see how sometimes the curveballs were responsible
for wonderful experiences that I would never have had
without the unexpected twists and turns.

I felt moved to write this chapter because I am 68 years old, and I feel that my life has a very different "feel" than it did before I was a senior. I do want to point out that there are as many different ways people do senior living as there are seniors in this world, but if sharing some of my experiences and points of view in this chapter helps you or even gives you a chuckle, then I've accomplished my mission.

In the first eight chapters of this book, I write about specific areas that I believe are important for us to reflect on when choosing to live with simplicity. Our understanding of these different aspects of our lives may change over time, so reflecting on them as seniors may be beneficial to us. I invite you to review the worksheets at the end of each chapter and reflect on each of the aspects of your life, perhaps in a new way.

If I were to define "living with simplicity," I would say that it's living my life as simply and as uncluttered as possible, with peace and calm. I'm not just talking about physical clutter like with my possessions but also about decluttering my understanding in these areas of my life: What do I value in my life, and how do I incorporate it all in my daily living? Who am I?— Not an easy question to answer but well worth reflecting upon. Making certain that I have knowledge of the ins and outs of my finances. How do I choose to use my time? Working on my thoughts to be more positive. Understanding what gives my life meaning. How I allow my passion to flow through creativity, and how I take care of myself (my health).

My choice to live with simplicity slowly came into being after I moved into my tiny cottage on the southern coast of Maine, but my desire for simplicity has always been within me. Living with simplicity is both a decision and a choice we make. As I have said before, people live with simplicity in many different ways because it's very personal. We can live in a huge home and still live simply because I believe choosing to live this way is an inner expression of how we want to show up on this planet. I love keeping my life as simple as I can. I enjoy being present in each moment, and I appreciate the freedom to choose the pace of my life and how and with whom I spend my time. However, sometimes things happen, and we have to go through them as best we can, and hopefully we can return to our simple life sooner than later.

For example, I had two surgeries within eight months, as well as unexplainable swelling in my knees that is painful at times but mostly just stiff and difficult to get up and down from sitting. I'm also in need of cataract surgery, so I don't feel comfortable driving at night because I just can't see as well as I used to. When I came home from one of the surgeries—the major one (total shoulder joint replacement)—I kept hoping that I was just in a slump and things would get back to what I considered normal one of these days. And it felt like it took forever… After four months, I felt somewhat able to get back to my routine. Now, as I write this chapter, it's been nine months since the surgery and it continues to heal, and I feel like my "normal" life has changed a bit but I'm adjusting.

One specific part of becoming a senior that I had to learn to do is to seriously slow down the pace of my life so that I can continue to be in the present moment without stress and anxiety. I was very active until just recently, in the past two years, when it occurred to me that I just couldn't continue a fast pace of living. I'll share an example of when I could manage a crazy-busy life. I had a family, a job, and I earned four academic degrees in 20 years (I was 50 years old when I graduated with my last degree). It took me a few years to learn to slow down after I stopped my formal education, but my pace was still quite fast and busy. Two years ago (when I was 66), while I was working part-time as a therapist, I created a program and started to launch it. I experienced quite a bit of anxiety as I was about to go with it, and a close friend reminded me that I really needed to slow down and stop doing so much. That was my moment of realization that I couldn't do this fast-paced living anymore. It was difficult to face that reality, but deep down I knew he was right. I did slow down, and it was the right thing to do. I realize, however, that I needed someone to tell me, otherwise I don't think I would have slowed down. The feelings I had after deciding to slow the pace of my life were very positive and freeing. I still work part-time as a therapist, but I limit any other major endeavors. I still make time to create, and this book is one of those creative expressions that I truly enjoy!

I've mentioned already in other chapters how our society values youth and productivity. I know many seniors who have shared with me that they feel useless because they can't work as fast and do as much as they used to—they feel unproductive. And we do have to get used to living in a world that values youth. Some cultures in the world value the wisdom of the elders, but not in my world. And so I am attempting to encourage seniors to consider being agreeable to slowing the pace of their lives *without guilt* as a gift to themselves and for their well-being.

Incorporating balance in our daily living is a good self-care tool. I have described the nine areas of living a balanced life in Chapter Eight. I will write them again in this chapter and include ideas specifically for seniors, and I ask that you carefully reflect on your life and see how you can incorporate some of these ideas if they seem helpful and if you haven't already.

My variation of the nine areas of a balanced life includes:

1. Our ability to **manage our use of time to best fit our pace** of living. When we get older, we just can't go as fast as we used to. I'm finding that if I am forced to go about my life too fast, it gives me anxiety or stresses me to the point of being annoyed. It's perfectly acceptable to opt out of invites from friends and family if you feel that it would be too much for you.

2. The next area is in choosing to **work or volunteer at positions that are complementary to our skills and interests**. Some seniors want to keep working, perhaps part-time, because they enjoy working. Some keep working because they have to for financial reasons. Either way, one might consider working in an area that feels fulfilling, a kind of work that you have passion for. It's the same for choosing volunteer work—find what you love to do and do it.

3. It's important that we **sleep enough hours so that we feel energized** and are able to get through our day. This may require going to bed earlier or perhaps talking with your doctor about sleeping aids. Sleep is very important to being healthy, so we need to take it seriously. I bought a small mat that goes under the mattress or between the topper and my mattress, and it's synced with my cell phone. In the morning, I look at the app on my phone and get a sleep report that includes my heart rate average, breathing disturbances (low, medium, or high), snoring times, and the percentage of my sleep in the categories of light, deep, or REM. This information helps me to know my sleep quality. The brand is Withings. I can't say that it's scientifically exact, but it gives me an idea of my sleep quality. If your doctor thinks you need something more for your health in sleeping, then follow the professional's suggestions.

4. We do need to take the time to **visit with family and/or friends who are kind and loving so that we have a healthy and enjoyable social life**. One of the biggest concerns that I have observed in working with seniors is that they are lonely, and some have lost the interest or ability to create a social life for themselves. It does not have to be daily outings, but at least once a week, it is important to take the time to visit with someone enjoyable to be with. I share ideas on how to find connections with others later in this chapter.

5. It is important to have time to **tend to our needs for intimacy or spending time with our significant other** if we have one. Not everyone has a significant other, but if you do, then take the initiative to spend quality time with each other. Seniors have the benefit of creating a variety of different types of relationships. Sometimes people each live in their own homes and are still a couple. We are adults and we can create whatever works for us in the area of intimate relationships.

6. Another important area is **taking the time to find meaning in our lives**, which includes allowing our creative juices to flow. Chapters Six and Seven are devoted to inviting and encouraging people to find their creative expressions and to make the time to do them. In this area, we can also include spiritual practices, religion, or other meaning-making activities that enrich our lives. It is important to figure out what your beliefs are about spirituality, and it's acceptable not to have any. However, finding what gives your life meaning and putting words to express and define it can be very helpful as we grow older.

7. It is also important to **be open and take time for personal growth/ education**. It's never too late to learn something new. There are many opportunities through local adult education programs and sometimes through our public libraries to attend a class on a topic that interests us. Some colleges offer free courses to seniors, so check those out as well.

8. Making the time for recreational/vacation adventures is also important in a balanced life. Most people can't wait to retire so they can travel, yet when they have the time to do so after retirement, they either feel overwhelmed with the idea or they don't know if they can afford it. Take local weekend trips to start exploring the world around you. Adventures are a wonderful way to spend time and explore new places and things.

9. Last but not least, it is **seriously important that we tend to our** health and wellness, beginning with eating nutritious food. I found it helpful to create my own cookbook with all my favorite recipes. I tend to forget the favorite dishes that I'm good at making, so I bought a thin three-ring binder and I either hand write or type up the recipes. I then place them in plastic cover sheets and accumulate them in the binder. I add new ones as I discover new dishes that I enjoy. I list the meals on the front of the binder by page number so they're easy to find. When it's time to decide next week's meals, I browse through the list. This is how I live with simplicity with my meals. Not much thinking goes into figuring out what my meals for the week will be. Other aspects of healthy living include a routine for daily exercise (such as a 20–30 minute daily walk) and yearly visits to your professional health care providers.

If we are able to spend time and effort in all these areas of our lives, I believe that we have a foundation to help us through those difficult times that creep up unexpectedly. Nonetheless, there are adjustments when we become a senior, and life is different than when we were younger. Having an open schedule when retired can be difficult to adjust to if we were accustomed to having a schedule when we were working, and perhaps we liked having this structure. Create a schedule now that you are retired so that you can accomplish what you want to on a daily basis. A realistic schedule may be helpful in motivating you to accomplish what you want to do *at your pace of comfort*. Going to bed and getting up every day at the same time, as well as eating your meals at the same time every day, is healthy for your body. Your schedule can include those fixed items, and then add in your exercise time and appointments with healthcare professionals. With the time left open, you can schedule your chores (cleaning your home, cooking, laundry, etc.), and don't forget to also schedule what makes you happy. For some of us, that might be meeting up with friends or acquaintances to have lunch. For others it's reading a book or going to the movies with a friend. Personally, I enjoy creating during my free time. If we were accustomed to having a schedule, it may be helpful to create one even though we are retired.

I understand that there are seniors who are social butterflies who have numerous friends, but not all people are in this category. When our friends are long-distance (because they moved to be closer to their families for support), we can talk to them on the phone, through email, text or the internet but it's not the same as spending time together and sharing activities and hugs.

Another adjustment that many of us experience is the loss of friends and family through death. My mother and I were close friends, and when she passed, 75 percent of my social life died with her. After some time passed, I spent a lot of time working on finding a new friend, and after a year, I did find a companion, and I continue to enjoy this friendship. Seniors who are married or partnered will eventually become single, and this loss is usually very deep and difficult. Loneliness and lack of social interaction have become a problem with seniors for all these various reasons. In fact, studies show that there are several medical and psychological issues that can affect a person who experiences loneliness and disconnection from other human beings.

When most of us were employed, we interacted with our coworkers, and we may have built friendships there. We may also have had school-aged children and found friendships with the parents of our children's friends. Now that we are not working anymore and our kids are grown and have their own families, our social connections may be lacking a bit. Some seniors belong to faith communities (churches, synagogues, mosques, spiritual centers), and usually these organizations are great with having social groups. They may also have specific ones for seniors. Other possible opportunities to find social connections include: Many communities (towns and cities) have senior groups that meet at a drop-in center where they can participate in scheduled activities, bus trips to restaurants, and other events. Sometimes local public libraries have groups that meet regularly and offer different events. Some people are shy and have a difficult time socializing with strangers, so remember that when you meet someone, they are no longer a stranger. I invite you to be open to social opportunities as they come up.

If you are new in town or have been out of circulation for a while because of health reasons, and you feel that it is difficult to reconnect to others and "make new friends," as I mentioned above, check in with your town office, city hall, or public library and ask about the local senior programs. Another idea for finding new friends or social connections is to join social clubs such as the Elks Club, Rotary Club, or other social clubs in your area. Simply look them up online and find out what the requirements are to join.

It is very important that we seek out social interactions with others, especially when we are not working, are retired, or are disabled and live alone. A very successful way that some people have adopted to experience connection with others is to volunteer for few hours a month or on a weekly basis. When we are able to reach out and touch someone else's life in a positive way, we both benefit from this simple human kindness.

I challenge you to reflect on your life and evaluate whether you are happy and whether your social needs are tended to. If not, please call your town/city hall or public library and see if they can point you in the right direction to find activities that you can attend and meet new people, where you can find connection with others. Do you feel like your life has balance in all the nine areas mentioned in this chapter? I invite you to reflect in your journal on each area of life mentioned and ponder the ideas for possibly improving some of these important aspects of your life. Also, keep in mind the possibility of volunteering to connect to a person who may benefit from a visit once in a while.

Lastly, I invite you to be open to getting professional help such as mental health therapy if you are having difficulty adjusting to these many changes. PsychologyToday.com is a good place to start looking for someone to talk to. You can find a therapist in your geographical area or opt to do Telehealth/internet sessions from home. Just be sure the provider you choose is licensed in your specific state. Each provider listed on PsychologyToday.com has information on what issues they work with and which insurances they are endorsed by (that they accept). You can also ask your primary care if they have a list of mental health therapists that they recommend. It's worth getting the help with someone experienced in working with seniors.

IN CLOSING

I truly hope that sharing my experiences and thoughts in this book has been helpful to you in some way. As I come to the end of my career, I felt moved to share some of my reflections on matters that I find very important in my own life. I wanted to bring forward discoveries that made a difference in my living a happy life rather than an unfulfilled one.

When I began to adopt the mindset of living with simplicity and discovering what matters in my life I was able to create my life to fit who I am, and in doing so I was able to find my passion and realize my purpose more clearly. I reflect back to when I was a young adult and how I had no idea of my abilities to make choices in my life that I felt were right for me. I am aware that there were many people my age, at that time, who knew how to make choices for themselves. But I also know from working with people in therapy for many years that there are many other individuals who were like me— unaware of their freedom to make choices in their lives that fit who they are and allows them to experience passion and joy.

Everything I shared in this book concerning myself, I did so as examples for the readers to understand the information I was trying to convey. I truly honor everyone's belief system, as well as everyone's source of meaning in their lives. The important thing is for everyone to know who they are, what they believe to be their truth, as well as what gives their lives meaning. When life brings us challenges, and we have a sense of self as well as know our truth and what gives our lives meaning, our challenges can be so much smoother.

I want to thank you for being willing to explore with me what *Living With Simplicity & Discovering What Matters* looks like. I hope you found something to help you on your life journey. I appreciate the opportunity in sharing with you my thoughts.